Cooking Space

100-Plus Recipes to Take the Stress Out of Cooking

- Alisha D. Campbell -

COTTAGELOAF.

If either the sponge or the dough be permitted to overwork itself, that is to say, if the mixing and kneading be neglected when it has reached the proper point for either, sour bread will probably be the consequence in warm weather, and bad bread in any. The goodness will also be endangered by placing it so near the fire as to make any part of it hot, instead of maintaining the gentle and equal degree of heat required for its due fermentation.

MILK OR BUTTER.—Milk which is not perfectly sweet will not only injure the flavour of the bread, but, in sultry weather, will often cause it to be quite uneatable; yet either of them, if *fresh and good*, will materially improve its quality.

To keep bread sweet and fresh, as soon as it is cold it should be put into a clean earthen pan, with a cover to it: this pan should be placed at a little distance from the ground, to allow a current of air to pass underneath. Some persons prefer keeping bread on clean wooden shelves without being covered, that the crust may not soften. Stale bread may be freshened by warming it through in a gentle oven. Stale pastry, cakes, &c., may also be improved by this method.

COTTAGELOAF.

The utensils required for making bread on a moderate scale, are a kneading-trough or pan, sufficiently large that the dough may be kneaded freely without throwing the flour over the edges, and also to allow for its rising; a hair sieve for straining yeast, and one or two strong spoons.

Yeast must always be good of its kind, and in a fitting state to produce ready and proper fermentation. Yeast of strong beer or ale produces more effect than that of milder kinds; and the fresher the yeast, the smaller the quantity will be required to raise the dough.

As a general rule, the oven for baking bread should be rather quick, and the heat so regulated as to penetrate the dough without hardening the outside. The oven door should not be opened after the bread is put in until the dough is set, or has become firm, as the cool air admitted, will have an unfavourable effect on it.

Brick ovens are generally considered the best adapted for baking bread: these should be heated with wood faggots, and then swept and mopped out, to cleanse them for the reception of the bread. Iron ovens are more difficult to manage, being apt to burn the surface of the bread before the middle is baked. To remedy this, a few clean bricks should be set at the bottom of the oven, close together, to receive the tins of bread. In many modern stoves the ovens are so much improved that they bake admirably; and they can always be brought to the required temperature, when it is higher than is needed, by leaving the door open for a time.

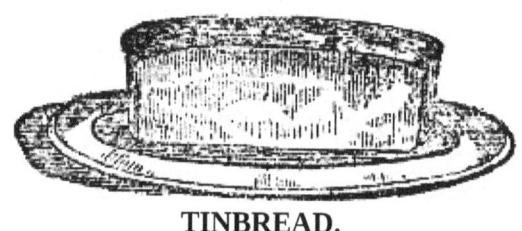

TINBREAD.

BREAD,tomakegoodHome-made(MissActon'   sRecipe).

Ingredients.—1 quartern of flour, 1 large tablespoonful of solid brewer's yeast, or nearly 1 oz. of fresh German yeast, 1¼ to 1½ pint of warm milk-and-water. *Mode.*—Put the flour into a large earthenware bowl or deep pan; then, with a strong metal or wooden spoon, hollow out the middle; but do not clear it entirely away from the bottom of the pan, as, in that case, the sponge, or leaven (as it was formerly termed) would stick to it, which it ought not to do. Next take either a large tablespoonful of brewer's yeast which has been rendered solid by mixing it with plenty of cold water, and letting it afterwards stand to settle for a day and night; or nearly an ounce of German yeast; put it into a large basin, and proceed to mix it, so that it shall be as smooth as cream, with ¾ pint of warm milk-and-water, or with water only; though even a very little milk will much improve the bread. Pour the yeast into the hole made in the flour, and stir into it as much of that which lies round it as will make a thick batter, in which there must be no lumps. Strew plenty of flour on the top, throw a thick clean cloth over, and set it where the air is warm; but do not place it upon the kitchen fender, for it will become too much heated there. Look at it from time to time: when it has been laid for nearly an hour, and when the yeast has risen and broken through the flour, so that bubbles appear in it, you will know that it is ready to be made up into dough. Then place the pan on a strong chair, or dresser, or table, of convenient height; pour into the sponge the remainder of the warm milk-and-water; stir into it as much of the flour as you can with the spoon; then wipe it out clean with your fingers, and lay it aside. Next take plenty of the remaining flour, throw it on the top of the leaven, and begin, with the knuckles of both hands, to knead it well. When the flour is nearly all kneaded in, begin to draw the edges of the dough towards the middle, in order to mix the whole thoroughly; and when it is free from flour and lumps and crumbs, and does not stick to the hands when touched, it will be done, and may be covered with the cloth, and left to rise a second time. In ¾ hour look at it, and should it have swollen very much and begin to crack, it will be light enough to bake. Turn it then on to a paste-board or very clean dresser, and with a large sharp knife divide it in two; make it up quickly into loaves, and despatch it to the oven: make one or two incisions across the tops of the loaves, as they will rise more easily if this be done. If baked in tins or pans, rub them with a tiny piece of butter laid on a piece of clean paper, to prevent the dough from sticking to them. All bread should be turned upside down, or on its side, as soon as it is drawn from the oven: if this be neglected, the under part of the loaves will become wet and blistered from the steam, which cannot then escape from them. *To make the dough without setting a sponge*, merely mix the yeast with the greater part of the warm milk-and-water, and wet up the whole of the flour at once after a little salt has been stirred in, proceeding exactly, in every other respect, as in the directions just given. As the dough will *soften* in the rising, it should be made quite firm at first, or it will be too lithe by the time it is ready for the oven. *Time.*—To be left to rise an hour the first time, ¾ hour the second time; to be baked from 1 to 1¼ hour, or baked in one loaf from 1½ to 2 hours.

BREAD, to make a Peck of good.

Ingredients.—3 lbs. of potatoes, 6 pints of cold water, ½ pint of good yeast, a peck of flour, 2 oz. of salt. *Mode.*—Peel and boil the potatoes; beat them to a cream while warm; then add 1 pint of cold water, strain through a colander, and add to it ½ pint of good yeast, which should have been put in water over-night to take off its bitterness. Stir all well together with a wooden spoon, and pour the mixture into the centre of the flour; mix it to the substance of cream, cover it over closely, and let it remain near the fire for an hour; then add the 5 pints of water, milk-warm, with 2 oz. of salt; pour this in, and mix the whole to a nice light dough. Let it remain for about 2 hours; then make it into 7 loaves, and bake for about 1½ hour in a good oven. When baked, the bread should weigh nearly 20 lbs. *Time.*—About 1½ hour.

BREAD-AND-BUTTER FRITTERS.

Ingredients.—Batter, 8 slices of bread and butter, 3 or 4 tablespoonfuls of jam. *Mode.*—Make a batter, the same as for apple fritters; cut some slices of bread and butter, not very thick; spread half of them with any jam that may be preferred, and cover with the other slices; slightly press them together, and cut them out in square, long, or round pieces. Dip them in the batter, and fry in boiling lard for about 10 minutes; drain them before the fire on a piece of blotting-paper or cloth. Dish them, sprinkle over sifted sugar, and serve. *Time.*—About 10 minutes. *Average cost*, 1s. *Sufficient* for 4 or 5 persons. *Seasonable* at any time.

BREAD-AND-BUTTER PUDDING, Baked.

Ingredients.—9 thin slices of bread and butter, 1½ pint of milk, 4 eggs, sugar to taste, ¼ lb. of currants, flavouring of vanilla, grated lemon-peel, or nutmeg. *Mode.*—Cut 9 slices of bread and butter, not very thick, and put them into a pie-dish, with currants between each layer, and on the top. Sweeten and flavour the milk, either by infusing a little lemon-peel in it, or essence of vanilla; well whisk the eggs, and stir ... strain this over the bread and butter, and bake in a ... for 1 hour, or rather longer. This pudding may be very much ... by adding cream, candied peel, or more eggs than stated above. It ... uld not be turned out, but sent to table in the pie-dish, and is better for being made about two hours before it is baked. *Time.*—1 hour, or rather longer. *Average cost*, 9d. *Sufficient* for 6 or 7 persons. *Seasonable* at any time.

BREADCRUMBS, Fried.

Cut the bread into thin slices, place them in a cool oven over-night, and when thoroughly dry and crisp, roll them down into fine crumbs. Put some lard, or clarified dripping, into a frying-pan; bring it to the boiling-point, throw in the crumbs, and fry them very quickly. Directly they are done, lift them out with a slice, and drain them before the fire from all greasy moisture. When quite crisp, they are ready for use. The fat they are fried in should be clear, and the crumbs should not have the slightest appearance or taste of having been, in the least degree, burnt.

BREAD, Fried, for Borders.

Proceed by frying some slices of bread, cut in any fanciful shape, in boiling lard. When quite crisp, dip one side of the sippet into the beaten white of an egg mixed with a little flour, and place it on the edge of the dish. Continue in this manner till the border is completed, arranging the sippets a pale and a dark one alternately.

BREAD, Fried Sippets of, for Garnishing many Dishes.

Cut the bread into thin slices, and stamp them out in whatever shape you like,—rings, crosses, diamonds, &c. &c. Fry them in the same manner as the bread-crumbs, in clear boiling lard or clarified dripping, and drain them until thoroughly crisp before the fire. When variety is desired, fry some of a pale colour, and others of a darker hue.

BREAKFASTS.

It will not be necessary to give here a long bill of fare of cold joints, &c., which may be placed on the sideboard, and do duty at the breakfast-table. Suffice it to say, that any cold meat the larder may furnish should be nicely garnished and be placed on the buffet. Collared and potted meats or fish, cold game or poultry, veal-and-ham pies, game-and-rump-steak pies, are all suitable dishes for the breakfast-table; as also cold ham, tongue, &c. &c.

The following list of hot dishes may perhaps assist our readers in knowing what to provide for the comfortable meal called breakfast. Broiled fish, such as mackerel, whiting, herrings, dried haddocks, &c.; mutton chops and rump-steaks, broiled sheep's kidneys, kidneys à la maître d'hôtel, sausages, plain rashers of bacon, bacon and poached eggs, ham and poached eggs, omelets, plain boiled eggs, œufs-au-plat, poached eggs on toast, muffins, toast, marmalade, butter, &c. &c.

In the summer, and when they are obtainable, always have a vase of freshly-gathered flowers on the breakfast-table, and, when convenient, a nicely-arranged dish of fruit: when strawberries are in season, these are particularly refreshing; as also grapes, or even currants.

BRILL.

Ingredients.—¼ lb. of salt to each gallon of water; a little vinegar. *Mode.*—Clean the brill, cut off the fins, and rub it over with a little lemon-juice, to preserve its whiteness. Set the fish in sufficient cold water to cover it; throw in salt, in the above proportions, and a little vinegar, and bring it gradually to boil: simmer very gently, till the fish is done, which will be in about 10 minutes for a small brill, reckoning from the time the water begins to simmer. It is difficult to give the *exact* number of minutes required for cooking a brill, as the fish varies somewhat in thickness, but the cook can always bear in mind that fish of every description should be *verythor oughly dressed*, and never come to table in the *least degree underdone*. The time for boiling of course depends entirely on the size of the fish. Serve it on a hot napkin, and garnish with cut lemon, parsley, horseradish, and a little lobster coral sprinkled over the fish. Send lobster or shrimp sauce and plain melted butter to table with it. *Time.*—After the water boils, a small brill, 10 minutes; a medium sized brill, 15 to 20 minutes; a large brill, ½ hour.

Average cost, from 4*s.* to 8*s.*; but when the market is plentifully supplied, may be had from 2*s.* each. *Seasonable* from August to April.

To choose Brill. —The flesh of this fish, like that of turbot, should be of a yellowish tint, and should be chosen on account of its thickness. If the flesh has a bluish tint, it is not good.

A Brill and John Dory are carved in the same manner as a Turbot.

Note.—The thick parts of the middle of the back are the best slices in a turbot; and the rich gelatinous skin covering the fish, as well as a little of the thick part of the fins, are dainty morsels, and should be placed on each plate.

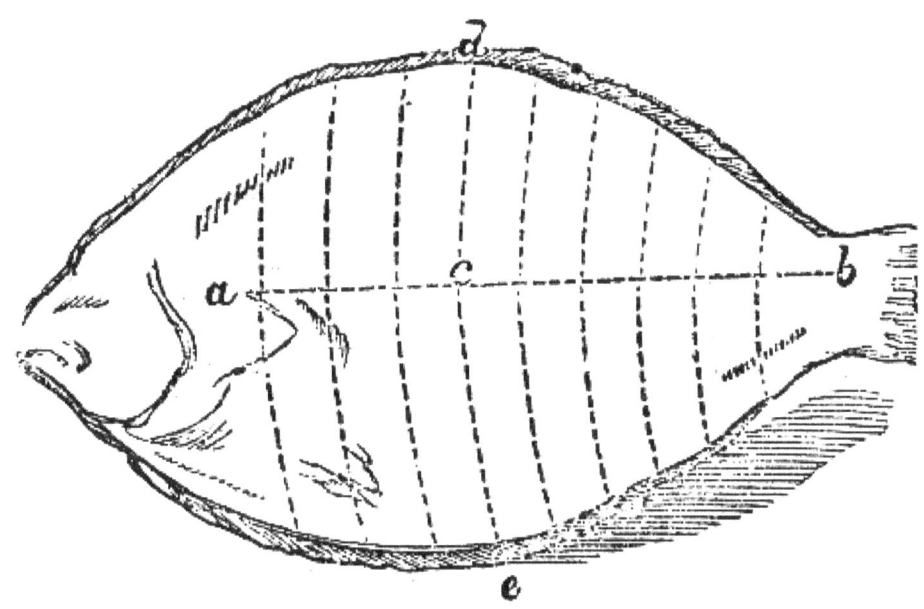

HOW TO CARVE A BRILL.

BROWNING, for Stock.

Ingredients.—2 oz. of powdered sugar, and ½ a pint of water. *Mode.*—Place the sugar in a stewpan over a slow fire until it begins to melt, keeping it stirred with a wooden spoon until it becomes black, when add the water, and let it dissolve. Cork closely, and use a few drops when required.

Note.—In France, burnt onions are made use of for the purpose of browning. As a general rule, the process of browning is to be discouraged, as apt to impart a slightly unpleasant flavour to the stock, and consequently all soups made from it.

BROWNINGforGraviesandSauces.

The browning for stock answers equally well for sauces and gravies, when it is absolutely necessary to colour them in this manner; but where they can be made to look brown by using ketchup, wine, browned flour, tomatoes, or any coloured sauce, it is far preferable. As, however, in cooking so much depends on appearance, perhaps it would be as well for the inexperienced cook to use the artificial means. When no browning is at hand, and you wish to heighten the colour of your gravy, dissolve a lump of sugar in an iron spoon close to a sharp fire; when it is in a liquid state, drop it into the sauce or gravy quite hot. Care, however, must be taken not to put in too much, as it would impart a very disagreeable flavour to the preparation.

BRUSSELS-SPROUTS,Boiled.

Ingredients.—To each ½ gallon of water allow 1 heaped tablespoonful of salt; a *very small* piece of soda. *Mode.*—Clean the sprouts from insects, nicely wash them, and pick off any dead or discoloured leaves from the outsides; put them into a saucepan of *boiling* water, with salt and soda in the above proportion; keep the pan uncovered, and let them boil quickly over a brisk fire until tender; drain, dish, and serve with a tureen of melted butter, or with a maître d'hôtel sauce poured over them. Another mode of serving them is, when they are dished, to stir in about 1½ oz. of butter and a seasoning of pepper and salt. They must, however, be sent to table very quickly, as, being so very small, this vegetable soon cools. Where the cook is very expeditious, this vegetable when cooked may be arranged on the dish in the form of a pineapple, and so served has a very pretty appearance. *Time.*—from 9 to 12 minutes after the water boils. *Averagecost* , 1*s*. 4*d*. per peck. *Sufficient.*—Allow between 40 and 50 for 5 or 6 persons. *Seasonable* from November to March.

BUBBLE-AND-SQUEAK.

[COLD MEAT COOKERY.] *Ingredients.*—A few thin slices of cold boiled beef; butter, cabbage, 1 sliced onion, pepper and salt to taste. *Mode.*—Fry the slices of beef gently in a little butter, taking care not to dry them up. Lay them on a flat dish, and cover with fried greens. The greens may be prepared from cabbage sprouts or green savoys. They should be boiled till tender, well drained, minced, and placed, till quite hot, in a frying-pan, with butter, a sliced onion, and seasoning of pepper and salt. When the onion is done, it is ready to serve. *Time.*—Altogether, ½ hour. *Average cost*, exclusive of the cold beef, 3*d*. *Seasonable* at any time.

BULLOCK'S HEART, to Dress.

Ingredients.—1 heart, stuffing of veal forcemeat. *Mode.*—Put the heart into warm water to soak for 2 hours; then wipe it well with a cloth, and, after cutting off the lobes, stuff the inside with a highly-seasoned forcemeat. Fasten it in, by means of a needle and coarse thread; tie the heart up in paper, and set it before a good fire, being very particular to keep it well basted, or it will eat dry, there being very little of its own fat. Two or three minutes before dishing remove the paper, baste well, and serve with good gravy and red-currant jelly or melted butter. If the heart is very large, it will require 2 hours, and, covered with a caul, may be baked as well as roasted. *Time.*—Large heart, 2 hours. *Average cost*, 2*s*. 6*d*. *Sufficient* for 6 or 8 persons. *Seasonable* all the year.

Note.—This is an excellent family dish, is very savoury, and, though not seen at many good tables, may be recommended for its cheapness and economy.

BUNS, Light.

Ingredients.—½ teaspoonful of tartaric acid, ½ teaspoonful of bicarbonate of soda, 1 lb. of flour, 2 oz. of butter, 2 oz. of loaf sugar, ¼ lb. of currants or raisins,—when liked, a few caraway seeds, ½ pint of cold new milk, 1 egg. *Mode.*—Rub the tartaric acid, soda, and flour all together through a hair sieve; work the butter into the flour; add the sugar, currants, and caraway seeds, when the flavour of the latter is liked. Mix all these ingredients well together; make a hole in the middle of the flour, and pour in the milk, mixed with the egg, which should be well beaten; mix quickly, and set the dough, with a fork, on baking-tins, and bake the buns for about 20 minutes. This mixture makes a very good cake, and if put into a tin, should be baked 1½ hour. The same quantity of flour, soda, and tartaric acid, with ½ pint of milk and a little salt, will make either bread or tea-cakes, if wanted quickly. *Time.*—20 minutes for the buns; if made into a cake, 1½ hour. *Sufficient* to make about 12 buns.

BUNS.

BUNS, Plain.

Ingredients.—1 lb. of flour, 6 oz. of good butter, ¼ lb. of sugar, 1 egg, nearly ¼ pint of milk, 2 small teaspoonfuls of baking-powder, a few drops of essence of lemon. *Mode.*—Warm the butter, without oiling it; beat it with a wooden spoon; stir the flour in gradually with the sugar, and mix these ingredients well together. Make the milk lukewarm, beat up with it the yolk of the egg and the essence of lemon, and stir these to the flour, &c. Add the baking-powder, beat the dough well for about 10 minutes, divide it into 24 pieces, put them into buttered tins or cups, and bake in a brisk oven from 20 to 30 minutes. *Time.*—20 to 30 minutes. *Average cost*, 1s. *Sufficient* to make 12 buns. *Seasonable* at any time.

BUNS, V ictoria.

Ingredients.—2 oz. of pounded loaf sugar, 1 egg, 1½ oz. of ground rice, 2 oz. of butter, 1½ oz. of currants, a few thin slices of candied-peel, flour. *Mode.*—Whisk the egg, stir in the sugar, and beat these ingredients both together; beat the butter to a cream, stir in the ground rice, currants, and candied-peel, and as much flour as will make it of such a consistency that it may be rolled into 7 or 8 balls. Place these on a buttered tin, and bake them for ½ to ¾ hour. They should be put into the oven immediately or they will become heavy, and the oven should be tolerably brisk. *Time.*—½ to ¾ hour. *Averagecost*, 6d. *Sufficient* to make 7 or 8 buns. *Seasonable* at any time.

BUTTER, Br owned.

Ingredients.—¼ lb. of butter, 1 tablespoonful of minced parsley, 3 tablespoonfuls of vinegar, salt and pepper to taste. *Mode.*—Put the butter into a frying pan over a nice clear fire, and when it smokes, throw in the parsley, and add the vinegar and seasoning. Let the whole simmer for a minute or two, when it is ready to serve. This is a very good sauce for skate. *Time.*—¼ hour.

BUTTER, Clarified.

Put the butter in a basin before the fire, and when it melts, stir it round once or twice, and let it settle. Do not strain it unless absolutely necessary, as it causes so much waste. Pour it gently off into a clean dry jar, carefully leaving all sediment behind. Let it cool, and carefully exclude the air by means of a bladder, or piece of wash-leather, tied over. If the butter is salt, it may be washed before melting, when it is to be used for sweet dishes.

BUTTER, Curled.

Tie a strong cloth by two of the corners to an iron hook in the wall; make a knot with the other two ends, so that a stick might pass through. Put the butter into the cloth; twist it tightly over a dish, into which the butter will fall through the knot, so forming small and pretty little strings. The butter may then be garnished with parsley, if to serve with a cheese course; or it may be sent to table plain for breakfast, in an ornamental dish. Squirted butter for garnishing hams, salads, eggs, &c., is made by forming a piece of stiff paper in the shape of a cornet, and squeezing the butter in fine strings from the hole at the bottom. Scooped butter is made by dipping a teaspoon or scooper in warm water, and then scooping the butter quickly and thin. In warm weather, it would not be necessary to heat the spoon.

BUTTER, Fairy.

Ingredients.—The yolks of 2 hard-boiled eggs, 1 tablespoonful of orange-flower water, 2 tablespoonfuls of pounded sugar, ¼ lb. of good fresh butter. *Mode.*—Beat the yolks of the eggs smoothly in a mortar, with the orange-flower water and the sugar, until the whole is reduced to a fine paste; add the butter, and force all through an old but clean cloth by wringing the cloth and squeezing the butter very hard. The butter will then drop on the plate in large and small pieces, according to the holes in the cloth. Plain butter may be done in the same manner, and is very quickly prepared, besides having a very good effect.

BUTTER, to keep Fresh.

Butter may be kept fresh for ten or twelve days by a very simple process. Knead it well in cold water till the buttermilk is extracted; then put it in a glazed jar, which invert in another, putting into the latter a sufficient quantity of water to exclude the air. Renew the water every day.

BUTTER, Maître d'Hôtel, for putting into Broiled Fish just before it is sent to Table.

Ingredients.—¼ lb. of butter, 2 dessertspoonfuls of minced parsley, salt and pepper to taste, the juice of 1 large lemon. *Mode.*—Work the above ingredients well together, and let them be thoroughly mixed with a wooden spoon. If this is used as a sauce, it may be poured either under or over the meat or fish it is intended to be served with. *Average cost*, for this quantity, 5*d.*

Note.—4 tablespoonfuls of Béchamel, 2 do. of white stock, with 2 oz. of the above maître d'hôtel butter stirred into it, and just allowed to simmer for 1 minute, will be found an excellent hot maître d'hôtel sauce.

BUTTER, Melted.

Ingredients.—¼ lb. of butter, a dessertspoonful of flour, 1 wineglassful of water, salt to taste. *Mode.*—Cut the butter up into small pieces, put it into a saucepan, dredge over the flour, and add the water and a seasoning of salt; stir it *one way* constantly till the whole of the ingredients are melted and thoroughly blended. Let it just boil, when it is ready to serve. If the butter is to be melted with cream, use the same quantity as of water, but omit the flour; keep stirring it, but do not allow it to boil. *Time.*—1 minute to simmer. *Average cost* for this quantity, 4*d.*

BUTTER, Melted (more Economical).

Ingredients.—2 oz. of butter, 1 dessertspoonful of flour, salt to taste, ½ pint of water. *Mode.*—Mix the flour and water to a smooth batter, which put into a saucepan. Add the butter and a seasoning of salt, keep stirring *one way* till all the ingredients are melted and perfectly smooth; let the whole boil for a minute or two, and serve. *Time.*—2 minutes to simmer. *Average cost* for this quantity, 2*d.*

BUTTER, Rancid, What to do with.

When butter has become very rancid, it should be melted several times by a moderate heat, with or without the addition of water, and as soon as it has been well kneaded, after the cooling, in order to extract any water it may have retained, it should be put into brown freestone pots, sheltered from the contact of the air. The French often add to it, after it has been melted, a piece of toasted bread, which helps to destroy the tendency of the butter to rancidity.

BUTTER, Melted (the French Sauce Blanche).

Ingredients.—¼ lb. of fresh butter, 1 tablespoonful of flour, salt to taste, ½ gill of water, ½ spoonful of white vinegar, a very little grated nutmeg. *Mode.*—Mix the flour and water to a smooth batter, carefully rubbing down with the back of a spoon any lumps that may appear. Put it in a saucepan with all the other ingredients, and let it thicken on the fire, but do not allow it to boil, lest it should taste of the flour. *Time.*—1 minute to simmer. *Average cost*, 5*d.* for this quantity.

BUTTER, Melted, made with Milk.

Ingredients.—1 teaspoonful of flour, 2 oz. of butter, ½ pint of milk, a few grains of salt. *Mode.*—Mix the butter and flour smoothly together on a plate, put it into a lined saucepan, and pour in the milk. Keep stirring it *one way* over a sharp fire; let it boil quickly for a minute or two, and it is ready to serve. This is a very good foundation for onion, lobster, or oyster sauce: using milk instead of water makes it look much whiter and more delicate. *Time.*—Altogether, 10 minutes. *Average cost* for this quantity, 3*d.*

CABBAGE, Boiled.

Ingredients.—To each ½ gallon of water allow 1 heaped tablespoonful of salt; a *very small* piece of soda. *Mode.*—Pick off all the dead outside leaves, cut off as much of the stalk as possible, and cut the cabbages across twice, at the stalk end; if they should be very large, quarter them. Wash them well in cold water, place them in a colander, and drain; then put them into *plenty* of *fast-boiling* water, to which have been added salt and soda in the above proportions. Stir them down once or twice in the water, keep the pan uncovered, and let them boil quickly until tender. The instant they are done, take them up into a colander, place a plate over them, let them thoroughly drain, dish, and serve. *Time.*—Large cabbages, or savoys, ½ to ¾ hour, young summer cabbage, 10 to 12 minutes, after the water boils. *Average cost*, 2d. each in full season. *Sufficient.*—2 large ones for 4 or 5 persons. *Seasonable.*—Cabbages and sprouts of various kinds at any time.

CABBAGE, Red, Pickled.

Ingredients.—Red cabbages, salt and water; to each quart of vinegar, ½ oz. of ginger well bruised, 1 oz. of whole black pepper, and, when liked, a little cayenne. *Mode.*—Take off the outside decayed leaves of a nice red cabbage, cut it in quarters, remove the stalks, and cut it across in very thin slices. Lay these on a dish, and strew them plentifully with salt, covering them with another dish. Let them remain for 24 hours, turn into a colander to drain, and, if necessary, wipe lightly with a clean soft cloth. Put them in a jar; boil up the vinegar with spices in the above proportion, and, when cold, pour it over the cabbage. It will be fit for use in a week or two, and, if kept for a very long time, the cabbage is liable to get soft and to discolour. To be really nice and crisp, and of a good red colour, it should be eaten almost immediately after it is made. A little bruised cochineal boiled with the vinegar adds much to the appearance of this pickle. Tie down with bladder, and keep in a dry place. *Seasonable* in July and August, but the pickle will be much more crisp if the frost has just touched the leaves.

CABBAGE, Red, Stewed.

Ingredients.—1 red cabbage, a small slice of ham, ½ oz. of fresh butter, 1 pint of weak stock or broth, 1 gill of vinegar, salt and pepper to taste, 1 tablespoonful of pounded sugar. *Mode.*—Cut the cabbage into very thin slices, put it into a stewpan, with the ham cut in dice, the butter, ½ pint of stock, and the vinegar; cover the pan closely, and let it stew for 1 hour. When it is very tender, add the remainder of the stock, a seasoning of salt and pepper, and the pounded sugar; mix all well together, stir over the fire until nearly all the liquor is dried away, and serve. Fried sausages are usually sent to table with this dish: they should be laid round and on the cabbage, as a garnish. *Time.*—Rather more than 1 hour. *Average cost,* 4*d.* each. *Sufficient* for 4 persons. *Seasonable* from September to January.

CABBAGE SOUP.

Ingredients.—1 large cabbage, 3 carrots, 2 onions, 4 or 5 slices of lean bacon, salt and pepper to taste, 2 quarts of medium stock. *Mode.*—Scald the cabbage, cut it up and drain it. Line the stewpan with the bacon, put in the cabbage, carrots, and onions; moisten with skimmings from the stock, and simmer very gently, till the cabbage is tender; add the stock, stew softly for half an hour, and carefully skim off every particle of fat. Season and serve. *Time.*—1½ hour. *Average cost*, 1*s.* per quart. *Seasonable* in winter. *Sufficient* for 8 persons.

CABINET or CHANCELLOR'S PUDDING.

Ingredients.—1½ oz. of candied peel, 4 oz. of currants, 4 dozen sultanas, a few slices of Savoy cake, sponge-cake, a French roll, 4 eggs, 1 pint of milk, grated lemon-rind, ¼ nutmeg, 3 tablespoonfuls of sugar. *Mode.*—Melt some butter to a paste, and with it, well grease the mould or basin in which the pudding is to be boiled, taking care that it is buttered in every part. Cut the peel into thin slices, and place these in a fanciful device at the bottom of the mould, and fill in the spaces between with currants and sultanas; then add a few slices of sponge-cake or French roll; drop a few drops of melted butter on these, and between each layer sprinkle a few currants. Proceed in this manner until the mould is nearly full; then flavour the milk with nutmeg and grated lemon-rind; add the sugar, and stir to this the eggs, which should be well beaten. Beat this mixture for a few minutes; then strain it into the mould, which should be quite full; tie a piece of buttered paper over it, and let it stand for two hours; then tie it down with a cloth, put it into boiling water, and let it boil slowly for 1 hour. In taking it up, let it stand for a minute or two before the cloth is removed; then quickly turn it out of the mould or basin, and serve with sweet sauce separately. The flavouring of this pudding may be varied by substituting for the lemon-rind essence of vanilla or bitter almonds; and it may be made much richer by using cream; but this is not at all necessary. *Time.*—1 hour, *Average cost*, 1*s*. 3*d*. *Sufficient* for 5 or 6 persons. *Seasonable* at any time.

CABINETPUDDING.

CABINETorBOILEDBREAD-AND-BUTTERPUDDING, Plain.

Ingredients.—2 oz. of raisins, a few thin slices of bread and butter, 3 eggs, 1 pint of milk, sugar to taste, ¼ nutmeg. *Mode.*—Butter a pudding-basin and line the inside with a layer of raisins that have been previously stoned; then nearly fill the basin with slices of bread and butter with the crust cut off, and, in another basin, beat the eggs; add to them the milk, sugar, and grated nutmeg; mix all well together, and pour the whole on to the bread and butter; let it stand ½ hour, then tie a floured cloth over it; boil for 1 hour, and serve with sweet sauce. Care must be taken that the basin is quite full before the cloth is tied over. *Time.*—1 hour. *Average cost*, 9*d*. *Sufficient* for 5 or 6 persons. *Seasonable* at any time.

CAFÉAULAIT .

This is merely very strong coffee added to a large proportion of good hot milk; about 6 tablespoonfuls of strong coffee being quite sufficient for a breakfast-cupful of milk. Of the essence which answers admirably for *café au lait*, so much would not be required. This preparation is infinitely superior to the weak watery coffee so often served at English tables. A little cream mixed with the milk, if the latter cannot be depended on for richness, improves the taste of the coffee, as also the richness of the beverage.

Sufficient.—6 tablespoonfuls of strong coffee, or 2 tablespoonfuls of the essence, to a breakfast-cupful of milk.

CAFÉ NOIR.

This is usually handed round after dinner, and should be drunk well sweetened, with the addition of a little brandy or liqueurs, which may be added or not at pleasure. The coffee should be made very strong, and served in very small cups, but never mixed with milk or cream. *Café noir* may be made of the essence of coffee by pouring a tablespoonful into each cup, and filling it up with boiling water. This is a very simple and expeditious manner of preparing coffee for a large party, but the essence for it must be made very good, and kept well corked until required for use.

CAKES, Making and Baking of.

Eggs should always be broken into a cup, the whites and yolks separated, and they should always be strained. Breaking the eggs thus, the bad ones may be easily rejected without spoiling the others, and so cause no waste. As eggs are used instead of yeast, they should be very thoroughly whisked; they are generally sufficiently beaten when thick enough to carry the drop that falls from the whisk.

Loaf Sugar should be well pounded, and then sifted through a fine sieve.

Currants should be nicely washed, picked, dried in a cloth, and then carefully examined, that no pieces of grit or stone may be left amongst them. They should then be laid on a dish before the fire, to become thoroughly dry; as, if added damp to the other ingredients, cakes will be liable to be heavy.

Good Butter should always be used in the manufacture of cakes; and, if beaten to a cream, it saves much time and labour to warm, but not melt, it before beating.

Less butter and eggs are required for cakes when yeast is mixed with the other ingredients.

The heat of the oven is of great importance, especially for large cakes. If the heat be not tolerably fierce, the batter will not rise. If the oven is too quick, and there is any danger of the cake burning or catching, put a sheet of clean paper over the top: newspaper, or paper that has been printed on, should never be used for this purpose.

To know when a cake is sufficiently baked, plunge a clean knife into the middle of it; draw it quickly out, and if it looks in the least sticky put the cake back, and close the oven door until the cake is done.

Cakes should be kept in closed tin canisters or jars, and in a dry place. Those made with yeast do not keep so long as those made without it.

CAKES, nice Breakfast.

Ingredients.—1 lb. of flour, ½ teaspoonful of tartaric acid, ½ teaspoonful of salt, ½ teaspoonful of carbonate of soda, 1½ breakfast-cupful of milk, 1 oz. of sifted loaf sugar, 2 eggs. *Mode.*—These cakes are made in the same manner as the soda bread, with the addition of eggs and sugar. Mix the flour, tartaric acid, and salt well together, taking care that the two latter ingredients are reduced to the finest powder, and stir in the sifted sugar, which should also be very fine. Dissolve the soda in the milk, add the eggs, which should be well whisked, and with this liquid work the flour, &c. into a light dough. Divide it into small cakes, put them into the oven immediately, and bake for about 20 minutes. *Time.*—20 minutes.

CAKE, Christmas.

Ingredients.—5 teacupfuls of flour, 1 teacupful of melted butter, 1 teacupful of cream, 1 teacupful of treacle, 1 teacupful of moist sugar, 2 eggs, ½ oz. of powdered ginger, ½ lb. of raisins, 1 teaspoonful of carbonate of soda, 1 tablespoonful of vinegar. *Mode.*—Make the butter sufficiently warm to melt it, but do not allow it to oil; put the flour into a basin, add to it the sugar, ginger, and raisins, which should be stoned and cut into small pieces. When these dry ingredients are thoroughly mixed, stir in the butter, cream, treacle, and well-whisked eggs, and beat the mixture for a few minutes. Dissolve the soda in the vinegar, add it to the dough, and be particular that these latter ingredients are well incorporated with the others;

put the cake into a buttered mould or tin, place it in a moderate oven immediately, and bake it from 1¾ to 2¼ hours. *Time.*—1¾ to 2¼ hours. *Average cost*, 1s. 6d.

CAKE, Common (suitable for sending to Children at School).

Ingredients.—2 lbs. of flour, 4 oz. of butter or clarified dripping, ½ oz. of caraway seeds, ¼ oz. of allspice, ½ lb. of pounded sugar, 1 lb. of currants, 1 pint of milk, 3 tablespoonfuls of fresh yeast. *Mode.*—Rub the butter lightly into the flour; add all the dry ingredients, and mix these well together. Make the milk warm, but not hot; stir in the yeast, and with this liquid mix the whole into a light dough; knead it well, and line the cake-tins with strips of buttered paper: this paper should be about 6 inches higher than the top of the tin. Put in the dough; stand it in a warm place to rise for more than an hour, then bake the cakes in a well-heated oven. If this quantity be divided into two, they will take from 1½ to 2 hours' baking, *Time.*—1½ to 2 hours. *Average cost*, 1s. 9d. *Sufficient* to make 2 moderate-sized cakes.

CAKE, Economical.

CAKE-MOULD.

Ingredients.—1 lb. of flour, ¼ lb. of sugar, ¼ lb. of butter or lard, ½ lb. of currants, 1 teaspoonful of carbonate of soda, the whites of 4 eggs, ½ pint of milk. *Mode.*—In making many sweet dishes, the whites of eggs are not required, and if well beaten and added to the above ingredients, make an excellent cake with or without currants. Beat the butter to a cream, well whisk the whites of the eggs, and stir all the ingredients together but the soda, which must not be added until all is well mixed, and the cake is ready to be put into the oven. When the mixture has been well beaten, stir in the soda, put the cake into a buttered mould, and bake it in a moderate oven for 1½ hour. *Time.*—1½ hour. *Average cost*, 1s. 3d.

CAKE, Good Holiday.

Ingredients.—1½d. worth of Borwick's German baking-powder, 2 lbs. of flour, 6 oz. of butter, ¼ lb. of lard, 1 lb. of currants, ½ lb. of stoned and cut raisins, ¼ lb. of mixed candied peel, ½ lb. of moist sugar, 3 eggs, ¾ pint of cold milk. *Mode.*—Mix the baking-powder with the flour; then rub in the butter and lard; have ready the currants, washed, picked, and dried, the raisins stoned and cut into small pieces (not chopped), and the peel cut into neat slices. Add these with the sugar to the flour, &c., and mix all the dry ingredients well together. Whisk the eggs, stir to them the milk, and with this liquid moisten the cake; beat it up well, that all may be very thoroughly mixed; line a cake-tin with buttered paper, put in the cake, and bake it from 2¼ to 2¾ hours in a good oven. To ascertain when it is done, plunge a clean knife into the middle of it, and if, on withdrawing it, the knife looks clean, and not sticky, the cake is done. To prevent it burning at the top, a piece of clean paper may be put over whilst the cake is soaking, or being thoroughly cooked in the middle. A steamer, such as is used for steaming potatoes, makes a very good cake-tin, if it be lined at the bottom and sides with buttered paper. *Time.*—2¼ to 2¾ hours. *Averagecost*, 2s. 6d. *Seasonable* at any time.

CAKE, Luncheon.

Ingredients.—½ lb. of butter, 1 lb. of flour, ½ oz. of caraway seeds, ¼ lb. of currants, 6 oz. of moist sugar, 1 oz. of candied peel, 3 eggs, ½ pint of milk, 1 small teaspoonful of carbonate of soda. *Mode.*—Rub the butter into the flour until it is quite fine; add the caraway seeds, currants (which should be nicely washed, picked, and dried), sugar, and candied peel cut into thin slices; mix these well together, and moisten with the eggs, which should be well whisked. Boil the milk, and add to it, whilst boiling, the carbonate of soda, which must be well stirred into it, and, with the milk, mix the other ingredients. Butter a tin, pour the cake into it, and bake it in a moderate oven from 1 to 1½ hour. *Time.*—1 to 1½ hour. *Average cost*, 1s. 8d. *Seasonable* at any time.

CAKE, a nice useful.

Ingredients.—¼ lb. of butter, 6 oz. of currants, ¼ lb. of sugar, 1 lb. of dried flour, 2 teaspoonfuls of baking-powder, 3 eggs, 1 teacupful of milk, 2 oz. of sweet almonds, 1 oz. of candied peel. *Mode.*—Beat the butter to a cream; wash, pick, and dry the currants; whisk the eggs; blanch and chop the almonds, and cut the peel into neat slices. When all these are ready, mix the dry ingredients together; then add the butter, milk, and eggs, and beat the mixture well for a few minutes. Put the cake into a buttered mould or tin, and bake it for rather more than 1½ hour. The currants and candied peel may be omitted, and a little lemon or almond flavouring substituted for them; made in this manner, the cake will be found very good. *Time.*—Rather more than 1½ hour. *Averagecost* , 1*s*. 9*d*.

CAKE,aPavini.

Ingredients.—1-2 lb. of flour, ½ lb. of ground rice, ½ lb. of raisins stoned and cut into small pieces, ¼ lb. of currants, ¼ lb. of butter, 2 oz. of sweet almonds, ¼ lb. of sifted loaf sugar, ½ nutmeg grated, 1 pint of milk, 1 teaspoonful of carbonate of soda. *Mode.*—Stone and cut the raisins into small pieces; wash, pick, and dry the currants; melt the butter to a cream, but without oiling it; blanch and chop the almonds, and grate the nutmeg. When all these ingredients are thus prepared, mix them well together; make the milk warm, stir in the soda, and with this liquid make the whole into a paste. Butter a mould, rather more than half fill it with the dough, and bake the cake in a moderate oven from 1½ to 2 hours, or less time should it be made into 2 cakes. *Time.*—1½ to 2 hours. *Average cost,* 1*s*. 8*d. Seasonable* at any time.

CAKE,anicePlain.

Ingredients.—1 lb. of flour, 1 teaspoonful of Borwick's baking-powder, ¼ lb. of good dripping, 1 teacupful of moist sugar, 3 eggs, 1 breakfast-cupful of milk, 1 oz. of caraway seeds, ½ lb. of currants. *Mode.*—Put the flour and the baking-powder into a basin; stir these together; then rub in the dripping, add the sugar, caraway seeds, and currants; whisk the eggs with the milk, and beat all together very thoroughly until the ingredients are well mixed. Butter a tin, put in the cake, and bake it from 1½ to 2 hours. Let the dripping be quite clean before using: to insure this, it is a good plan to clarify it. Beef dripping is better than any other for cakes, &c., as mutton dripping frequently has a very unpleasant flavour, which would be imparted to the preparation. *Time.*—1½ to 2 hours, *Average cost,* 1s. *Seasonable* at any time.

CAKE, a nice Plain, for Children.

Ingredients.—1 quartern of dough, ¼ lb. of moist sugar, ¼ lb. of butter or good beef dripping, ¼ pint of warm milk, ½ grated nutmeg or ½ oz. of caraway seeds. *Mode.*—It you are not in the habit of making bread at home, procure the dough from the baker's, and as soon as it comes in put it into a basin near the fire; cover the basin with a thick cloth, and let the dough remain a little while to rise. In the mean time, beat the butter to a cream, and make the milk warm; and when the dough has risen, mix with it thoroughly all the above ingredients, and knead the cake well for a few minutes. Butter some cake-tins, half fill them, and stand them in a warm place, to allow the dough to rise again. When the tins are three parts full, put the cakes into a good oven, and bake them from 1¾ to 2 hours. A few currants might be substituted for the caraway seeds when the flavour of the latter is disliked. *Time.*—1¾ to 2 hours. *Average cost*, 1s. 2d. *Seasonable* at any time.

CAKE, Queen.

Ingredients.—1 lb. of flour, ½ lb. of butter, ½ lb. of pounded loaf sugar, 3 eggs, 1 teacupful of cream, ½ lb. of currants, 1 teaspoonful of carbonate of soda, essence of lemon, or almonds to taste. *Mode.*—Work the butter to a cream; dredge in the flour, add the sugar and currants, and mix the ingredients well together. Whisk the eggs, mix them with the cream and flavouring, and stir these to the flour; add the carbonate of soda, beat the paste well for 10 minutes, put it into small buttered pans, and bake the cake from ¼ to ½ hour. Grated lemon-rind may be substituted for the lemon and almond flavouring, which will make the cakes equally nice. *Time.*—¼ to ½ hour. *Average cost*, 1s. 9d. *Seasonable* at any time.

CAKE, Saucer, for Tea.

Ingredients.—¼ lb. of flour, ¼ lb. of *tous-les-mois*, ¼ lb. of pounded white sugar, ¼ lb. of butter, 2 eggs, 1 oz. of candied orange or lemon-peel. *Mode.*—Mix the flour and *tous-les-mois* together; add the sugar, the candied peel cut into thin slices, the butter beaten to a cream, and the eggs well whisked. Beat the mixture for 10 minutes, put it into a buttered cake-tin or mould, or, if this is not obtainable, a soup-plate answers the purpose, lined with a piece of buttered paper. Bake the cake in a moderate oven from 1 to 1¼ hour, and when cold, put it away in a covered canister. It will remain good some weeks, even if it be cut into slices. *Time.*—1 to 1¼ hour. *Averagecost* , 1*s*. *Seasonable* at any time.

CAKES,Scrap.

Ingredients.—2 lbs. of leaf, or the inside fat of a pig; 1½ lb. of flour, ¼ lb. of moist sugar, ½ lb. of currants, 1 oz. of candied lemon-peel, ground allspice to taste. *Mode.*—Cut the leaf, or flead, as it is sometimes called, into small pieces; put it into a large dish, which place in a quick oven; be careful that it does not burn, and in a short time it will be reduced to oil, with the small pieces of leaf floating on the surface; and it is of these that the cakes should be made. Gather all the scraps together, put them into a basin with the flour, and rub them well together. Add the currants, sugar, candied peel, cut into thin slices, and the ground allspice. When all these ingredients are well mixed, moisten with sufficient cold water to make the whole into a nice paste; roll it out thin, cut it into shapes, and bake the cakes in a quick oven from 15 to 20 minutes. These are very economical and wholesome cakes for children, and the lard, melted at home, produced from the flead, is generally better than that you purchase. To prevent the lard from burning, and to insure its being a good colour, it is better to melt it in a jar placed in a saucepan of boiling water; by doing it in this manner, there will be no chance of its discolouring. *Time.*—15 to 20 minutes. *Sufficient* to make 3 or 4 dozen cakes. *Seasonable* from September to March.

CALF.

The manner of cutting up a calf for the English market is to divide the carcase into four quarters, with eleven ribs to each fore quarter; which are again subdivided into joints, as exemplified on the cut.

Hindquarter: —

    1. The loin.
    2. The chump, consisting of the rump and hock-bone.
    3. The fillet.
    4. The hock, or hind knuckle.

Forequarter: —

    5. The shoulder.
    6. The neck.
    7. The breast.
    8. The fore knuckle.

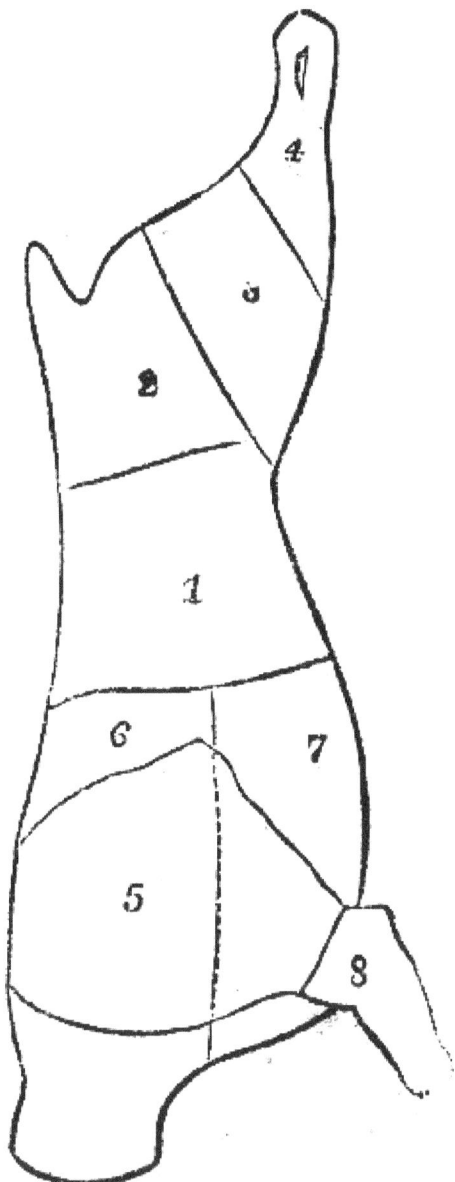

SIDE OF A CALF, SHOWING THE SEVERAL JOINTS.

The several parts of a moderately-sized well-fed calf, about eight weeks old, are nearly of the following weights:—loin and chump 18 lbs., fillet 12½ lbs., hind knuckle 5½ lbs., shoulder 11 lbs., neck 11 lbs., breast 9 lbs., and fore knuckle 5 lbs.; making a total of 144 lbs. weight. The London mode of cutting the carcase is considered better than that pursued in Edinburgh, as giving three roasting joints and one boiling in each quarter; besides the pieces being more equally divided, as regards flesh, and from the handsomer appearance they make on the table.

CALF'S FEET, Baked or Stewed.

Ingredients.—1 calf's foot, 1 pint of milk, 1 pint of water, 1 blade of mace, the rind of ½ lemon, pepper and salt to taste. *Mode.*—Well clean the foot, and either stew or bake it in the milk-and-water with the other ingredients from 3 to 4 hours. To enhance the flavour, an onion and a small quantity of celery may be added, if approved; ½ a teacupful of cream, stirred in just before serving, is also a great improvement to this dish. *Time.*—3 to 4 hours. *Average cost,* in full season, 9d. each. *Sufficient* for 1 person. *Seasonable* from March to October.

CALF'S FEET, Boiled, and Parsley and Butter.

Ingredients.—2 calf's feet, 2 slices of bacon, 2 oz. of butter, two tablespoonfuls of lemon-juice, salt and whole pepper to taste, 1 onion, a bunch of savoury herbs, 4 cloves, 1 blade of mace, water, parsley, and butter. *Mode.*—Procure 2 white calf's feet; bone them as far as the first joint, and put them into warm water to soak for 2 hours. Then put the bacon, butter, lemon-juice, onion, herbs, spices, and seasoning into a stewpan; lay in the feet, and pour in just sufficient water to cover the whole. Stew gently for about three hours; take out the feet, dish them, and cover with parsley and butter. The liquor they were boiled in should be strained and put by in a clean basin for use: it will be found very good as an addition to gravies, &c. *Time.*—Rather more than 3 hours. *Average cost,* in full season, 9d. each. *Sufficient* for 4 persons. *Seasonable* from March to October.

CALF'S-FOOT BROTH.

Ingredients.—1 calf's foot, 3 pints of water, 1 small lump of sugar, nutmeg to taste, the yolk of 1 egg, a piece of butter the size of a nut. *Mode.*—Stew the foot in the water with the lemon-peel *very gently*, until the liquid is half wasted, removing any scum, should it rise to the surface. Set it by in a basin until quite cold, then take off every particle of fat. Warm up about ½ pint of the broth, adding the butter, sugar, and a very small quantity of grated nutmeg; take it off the fire for a minute or two, then add the beaten yolk of the egg; keep stirring over the fire until the mixture thickens, but do not allow it to boil again after the egg is added, or it will curdle, and the broth will be spoiled. *Time.*—To be boiled until the liquid is reduced one half. *Average cost*, in full season, 9*d.* each. *Sufficient* to make 1½ pint of broth. *Seasonable* from March to October.

CALF'S FEET, Fricasseed.

Ingredients.—A set of calf's feet; for the batter, allow for each egg 1 tablespoonful of flour, 1 tablespoonful of bread-crumbs, hot lard, or clarified dripping, pepper and salt to taste. *Mode.*—If the feet are purchased uncleaned, dip them into warm water repeatedly, and scrape off the hair, first one foot and then the other, until the skin looks perfectly clean, a saucepan of water being kept by the fire until they are finished. After washing and soaking in cold water, boil them in just sufficient water to cover them, until the bones come easily away. Then pick them out, and after straining the liquor into a clean vessel, put the meat into a pie-dish until the next day. Now cut it down in slices about ½ inch thick, lay on them a stiff batter made of egg, flour, and bread-crumbs in the above proportion; season with pepper and salt, and plunge them into a pan of boiling lard. Fry the slices a nice brown, dry them before the fire for a minute or two, dish them on a napkin, and garnish with tufts of parsley. This should be eaten with melted butter, mustard, and vinegar. Be careful to have the lard boiling to *set* the batter, or the pieces of feet will run about the pan. The liquor they were boiled in should be saved, and will be found useful for enriching gravies, making jellies, &c. *Time.*—About 3 hours to stew the feet, 10 or 15 minutes to fry them. *Average cost*, in full season, 9*d.* each. *Sufficient* for 8 persons. *Seasonable* from March to October.

Note.—This dish can be highly recommended to delicate persons.

CALF'S-FEET JELLY.

Ingredients.—1 quart of calf's-feet stock, ½ lb. sugar, ½ pint of sherry, 1 glass of brandy, the shells and whites of 5 eggs, the rind and juice of 2 lemons, ½ oz. of isinglass. *Mode.*—Prepare the stock as directed in recipe for stock, taking care to leave the sediment, and to remove all the fat from the surface. Put it into a saucepan cold, without clarifying it; add the remaining ingredients, and stir them well together before the saucepan is placed on the fire. Then simmer the mixture gently for ¼ hour, *but do not stir it after it begins to warm.* Throw in a teacupful of cold water, boil for another 5 minutes, and keep the saucepan covered by the side of the fire for about ½ hour, but do not let it boil again. In simmering, the head or scum may be carefully removed as it rises; but particular attention must be given to the jelly, that it be not stirred in the slightest degree after it is heated. The isinglass should be added when the jelly begins to boil: this assists to clear it, and makes it firmer for turning out. Wring out a jelly-bag in hot water; fasten it on to a stand, or the back of a chair; place it near the fire with a basin underneath it, and run the jelly through it. Should it not be perfectly clear the first time, repeat the process until the desired brilliancy is obtained. Soak the moulds in water, drain them for half a second, pour in the jelly, and put it in a cool place to set. If ice is at hand, surround the moulds with it, and the jelly will set sooner, and be firmer when turned out. In summer it is necessary to have ice in which to put the moulds, or the cook will be, very likely, disappointed, by her jellies being in too liquid a state to turn out properly, unless a great deal of isinglass is used. When wanted for table, dip the moulds in hot water for a minute, wipe the outside with a cloth, lay a dish on the top of the mould, turn it quickly over, and the jelly should slip out easily. It is sometimes served broken into square lumps, and piled high in glasses. Earthenware moulds are preferable to those of pewter or tin for red jellies, the colour and transparency of the composition being often spoiled by using the latter. To make this jelly more economically, raisin wine may be substituted for the sherry and brandy, and the stock made from cow-heels, instead of calf's feet. *Time.*—20 minutes to simmer the jelly, ½ hour to stand covered. *Average cost,* reckoning the feet at 6*d.* each, 5*s.* 6*d. Sufficient* to fill two 1½-pint moulds. *Seasonable* at any time.

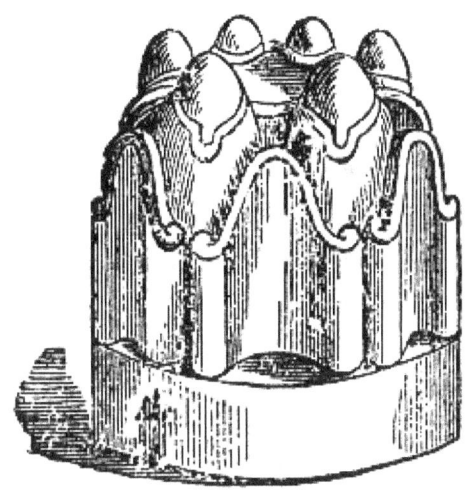
JELLY-MOULD.

Note.—As lemon-juice, unless carefully strained, is liable to make the jelly muddy, see that it is clear before it is added to the other ingredients. Omit the brandy when the flavour is objected to.

CALF'S HEAD à la Maître d'Hôtel.

[COLD MEAT COOKERY.] *Ingredients.*—The remains of a cold calf's head, rather more than ½ pint of maître d'hôtel sauce. *Mode.*—Make the sauce by the given recipe, and have it sufficiently thick that it may nicely cover the meat; remove the bones from the head, and cut the meat into neat slices. When the sauce is ready, lay in the meat; *gradually* warm it through, and, after it boils up, let it simmer very gently for 5 minutes, and serve. *Time.*—Rather more than 1½ hour. *Average cost*, exclusive of the meat, 1*s.* 2*d.* *Seasonable* from March to October.

CALF'S HEAD, Boiled (with the Skin on).

Ingredients.—Calf's head, boiling water, bread-crumbs, 1 large bunch of parsley, butter, white pepper and salt to taste, 4 tablespoonfuls of melted butter, 1 tablespoonful of lemon juice, 2 or 3 grains of cayenne. *Mode.*—Put the head into boiling water, and let it remain by the side of the fire for 3 or 4 minutes; take it out, hold it by the ear, and with the back of a knife, scrape off the hair (should it not come off easily, dip the head again into boiling water). When perfectly clean, take the eyes out, cut off the ears, and remove the brain, which soak for an hour in warm water. Put the head into hot water to soak for a few minutes, to make it look white, and then have ready a stewpan, into which lay the head; cover it with cold water, and bring it gradually to boil. Remove the scum, and add a little salt, which assists to throw it up. Simmer it very gently from 2½ to 3 hours, and when nearly done, boil the brains for ¼ hour; skin and chop them, not too finely, and add a tablespoonful of minced parsley which has been previously scalded. Season with pepper and salt, and stir the brains, parsley, &c., into about 4 tablespoonfuls of melted butter; add the lemon-juice and cayenne, and keep these hot by the side of the fire. Take up the head, cut out the tongue, skin it, put it on a small dish with the brains round it; sprinkle over the head a few bread-crumbs mixed with a little minced parsley; brown these before the fire, and serve with a tureen of parsley and butter, and either boiled bacon, ham, or pickled pork as an accompaniment. *Time.*—2½ to 3 hours. *Average cost*, according to the season, from 3*s*. to 7*s*. 6*d*. *Sufficient* for 8 or 9 persons. *Seasonable* from March to October.

CALF'S HEAD, Boiled (without the Skin).

Ingredients.—Calf's head, water, a little salt, 4 tablespoonfuls of melted butter, 1 tablespoonful of minced parsley, pepper and salt to taste, 1 tablespoonful of lemon-juice. *Mode.*—After the head has been thoroughly cleaned, and the brains removed, soak it in warm water to blanch it. Lay the brains also into warm water to soak, and let them remain for about an hour. Put the head into a stewpan, with sufficient cold water to cover it, and, when it boils, add a little salt; take off every particle of scum as it rises, and boil the head until perfectly tender. Boil the brains, chop them, and mix with them melted butter, minced parsley, pepper, salt, and lemon-juice in the above proportion. Take up the head, skin the tongue, and put it on a small dish with the brains round it. Have ready some parsley and butter, smother the head with it, and the remainder send to table in a tureen. Bacon, ham, pickled pork, or a pig's cheek, are indispensable with calf's head. The brains are sometimes chopped with hard-boiled eggs, and mixed with a little Béchamel or white sauce. *Time.*—From 1½ to 2¼ hours. *Average cost*, according to the season, from 3*s*. to 5*s*. *Sufficient* for 6 or 7 persons. *Seasonable* from March to October.

CALF'S HEAD.

HALF A CALF'S HEAD.

Note.—The liquor in which the head was boiled should be saved: it makes excellent soup, and will be found a nice addition to gravies, &c. Half a calf's head is as frequently served as a whole one, it being a more convenient-sized joint for a small family. It is cooked in the same manner, and served with the same sauces, as in the preceding recipe.

CALF'S HEAD, Collared.

Ingredients.—A calf's head, 4 tablespoonfuls of minced parsley, 4 blades of pounded mace, ½ teaspoonful of grated nutmeg, white pepper to taste, a few thick slices of ham, the yolks of 6 eggs boiled hard. *Mode.*—Scald the head for a few minutes; take it out of the water, and with a blunt knife scrape off all the hair. Clean it nicely, divide the head and remove the brains. Boil it tender enough to take out the bones, which will be in about 2 hours. When the head is boned, flatten it on the table, sprinkle over it a thick layer of parsley, then a layer of ham, and then the yolks of the eggs cut into thin rings and put a seasoning of pounded mace, nutmeg, and white pepper between each layer; roll the head up in a cloth, and tie it up as tightly as possible. Boil it for 4 hours, and when it is taken out of the pot, place a heavy weight on the top, the same as for other collared meats. Let it remain till cold; then remove the cloth and binding, and it will be ready to serve. *Time.*—Altogether, 6 hours. *Average cost*, 5s. to 7s. each. *Seasonable* from March to October.

CALF'S HEAD, Fricasseed (an Entrée).

[COLD MEAT COOKERY.] *Ingredients.*—The remains of a boiled calf's head, 1½ pint of the liquor in which the head was boiled, 1 blade of pounded mace, 1 onion minced, a bunch of savoury herbs, salt and white pepper to taste, thickening of butter and flour, the; yolks of 2 eggs, 1 tablespoonful of lemon-juice, forcemeat balls. *Mode.*—Remove all the bones from the head, and cut the meat into nice square pieces. Put 1½ pint of the liquor it was boiled in into a saucepan, with mace, onions, herbs, and seasoning in the above proportion: let this simmer gently for ¾ hour, then strain it and put in the meat. When quite hot through, thicken the gravy with a little butter rolled in flour, and, just before dishing the fricassee, put in the beaten yolks of eggs, and lemon-juice; but be particular, after these two latter ingredients are added, that the sauce does not boil, or it will curdle. Garnish with forcemeat balls and curled slices of broiled bacon. To insure the sauce being smooth, it is a good plan to dish the meat first, and then to add the eggs to the gravy: when these are set, the sauce may be poured over the meat. *Time.*—Altogether, 1¼ hour. *Average cost,* exclusive of the meat, 6*d*.

CALF'S HEAD, Hashed.

[COLD MEAT COOKERY.] *Ingredients.*—The remains of a cold boiled calf's head, 1 quart of the liquor in which it was boiled, a faggot of savoury herbs, 1 onion, 1 carrot, a strip of lemon-peel, 2 blades of pounded mace, salt and white pepper to taste, a very little cayenne, rather more than 2 tablespoonfuls of sherry, 1 tablespoonful of lemon-juice, 1 tablespoonful of mushroom ketchup, forcemeat balls. *Mode.*—Cut the meat into neat slices, and put the bones and trimmings into a stewpan with the above proportion of liquor that the head was boiled in. Add a bunch of savoury herbs, 1 onion, 1 carrot, a strip of lemon-peel, and 2 blades of pounded mace, and let these boil for 1 hour, or until the gravy is reduced nearly half. Strain it into a clean stewpan, thicken it with a little butter and flour, and add a flavouring of sherry, lemon-juice, and ketchup, in the above proportion; season with pepper, salt, and a little cayenne; put in the meat, let it *gradually* warm through, but not boil more than *two* or *three* minutes. Garnish the dish with forcemeat balls and pieces of bacon rolled and toasted, placed alternately, and send it to table very hot. *Time.*—Altogether

1½ hour. *Average cost*, exclusive of the remains of the head, 6*d*. *Seasonable* from March to October.

CALF'S HEAD, Moulded.

[COLD MEAT COOKERY.] *Ingredients.*—The remains of a calf's head, some thin slices of ham or bacon, 6 or 8 eggs boiled hard, 1 dessertspoonful of salt, pepper, mixed spice, and parsley, ½ pint of good white gravy. *Mode.*—Cut the head into thin slices. Butter a tin mould, cut the yolks of eggs in half, and put some of them round the tin; sprinkle some of the parsley, spice, &c., over it; then put in the head and the bacon in layers, adding occasionally more eggs and spice till the whole of the head is used. Pour in the gravy, cover the top with a thin paste of flour and water, and bake ¾ of an hour. Take off the paste, and, when cold, turn it out. *Time.*—From ¾ to 1 hour to bake the preparation. *Seasonable* from March to October.

CALF'S HEAD, to Carve.

This is not altogether the most easy-looking dish to cut when it is put before a carver for the first time; there is not much real difficulty in the operation, however, when the head has been attentively examined, and, after the manner of a phrenologist, you get to know its bumps, good and bad. In the first place, inserting the knife quite down to the bone, cut slices in the direction of the line 1 to 2; with each of these should be helped a piece of what is called the throat sweetbread, cut in the direction of from 3 to 4. The eye, and the flesh round, are favourite morsels with many, and should be given to those at the table who are known to be the greatest connoisseurs. The jawbone being removed, there will then be found some nice lean; and the palate, which is reckoned by some a tit-bit, lies under the head. On a separate dish there is always served the tongue and brains, and each guest should be asked to take some of these.

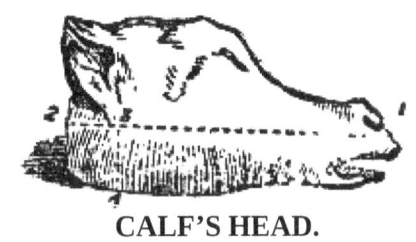

CALF'S HEAD.

CALF'S LIVER, aux Fines Herbes and Sauce Piquante.

Ingredients.—A calf's liver, flour, a bunch of savoury herbs, including parsley; when liked, 2 minced shalots; 1 teaspoonful of flour, 1 tablespoonful of vinegar, 1 tablespoonful of lemon-juice, pepper and salt to taste, ¼ pint water. *Mode.*—Procure a calf's liver as white as possible, and cut it into slices of a good and equal shape. Dip them in flour, and fry them of a good colour in a little butter. When they are done, put them on a dish, which keep hot before the fire. Mince the herbs very fine, put them in the frying-pan with a little more butter; add the remaining ingredients, simmer gently until the herbs are done, and pour over the liver. *Time.*—According to the thickness of the slices, from 5 to 10 minutes. *Average cost*, 10*d*. per lb. *Sufficient* for 7 or 8 persons. *Seasonable* from March to October.

CALF'S LIVER and BACON

Ingredients.—2 or 3 lbs. of liver, bacon, pepper and salt to taste, a small piece of butter, flour, 2 tablespoonfuls of lemon-juice, ¼ pint of water. *Mode.*—Cut the liver in thin slices, and cut as many slices of bacon as there are of liver; fry the bacon first, and put that on a hot dish before the fire. Fry the liver in the fat which comes from the bacon, after seasoning it with pepper and salt and dredging over it a very little flour. Turn the liver occasionally to prevent its burning, and when done, lay it round the dish with a piece of bacon between each. Pour away the bacon fat, put in a small piece of butter, dredge in a little flour, add the lemon-juice and water, give one boil, and pour it in the *middle* of the dish. It may be garnished with slices of cut lemon, or forcemeat balls. *Time.*—According to the thickness of the slices, from 5 to 10 minutes. *Average cost*, 10*d*. per lb. *Sufficient* for 6 or 7 persons. *Seasonable* from March to October.

CALF'S LIVER, Larded and Roasted (an Entrée).

Ingredients.—A calf's liver, vinegar, 1 onion, 3 or 4 sprigs of parsley and thyme, salt and pepper to taste, 1 bay-leaf, lardoons, brown gravy. *Mode.*—Take a fine white liver, and lard it the same as a fricandeau; put it into vinegar with an onion cut in slices, parsley, thyme, bay-leaf, and seasoning in the above proportion. Let it remain in this pickle for 24 hours, then roast and baste it frequently with the vinegar, &c.; glaze it, serve under it a good brown gravy, or sauce piquante, and send it to table very hot. *Time.*—Rather more than 1 hour. *Average cost*, 10*d.* per lb. *Sufficient* for 7 or 8 persons. *Seasonable* from March to October.

Note.—Calf's liver stuffed with forcemeat (*see* Forcemeat), to which has been added a little fat bacon, will be found a very savoury dish. It should be larded or wrapped in buttered paper, and roasted before a clear fire. Brown gravy and currant jelly should be served with it.

CAMP VINEGAR.

Ingredients.—1 head of garlic, ½ oz. cayenne, 2 teaspoonfuls of soy, 2 ditto walnut ketchup, 1 pint of vinegar, cochineal to colour. *Mode.*—Slice the garlic, and put it, with all the above ingredients, into a clean bottle. Let it stand to infuse for a month, when strain it off quite clear, and it will be fit for use. Keep it in small bottles well sealed, to exclude the air. *Average cost* for this quantity, 8*d.*

CANARY PUDDING (very good).

Ingredients.—The weight of 3 eggs in sugar and butter, the weight of 2 eggs in flour, the rind of 1 small lemon, 3 eggs. *Mode.*—Melt the butter to a liquid state, but do not allow it to oil; stir to this the sugar and finely-minced lemon-peel, and gradually dredge in the flour, keeping the mixture well stirred; whisk the eggs; add these to the pudding; beat all the ingredients until thoroughly blended, and put them into a buttered mould or basin; boil for 2 hours, and serve with sweet sauce. *Time.*—2 hours. *Average cost*, 9*d. Sufficient* for 4 or 5 persons. *Seasonable* at any time.

CANNELONS, or Fried Puffs (Sweet Entremets).

Ingredients.—½ lb. of puff-paste; apricot, or any kind of preserve that may be preferred; hot lard. *Mode.*—Cannelons, which are made of puff-paste rolled very thin, with jam inclosed, and cut out in long narrow rolls or puffs, make a very pretty and elegant dish. Make some good puff-paste by the recipe given; roll it out very thin, and cut it into pieces of an equal size, about 2 inches wide and 8 inches long; place upon each piece a spoonful of jam, wet the edges with the white of egg, and fold the paste over *twice*;

slightly press the edges together, that the jam may not escape in the frying; and when all are prepared, fry them in boiling lard until of a nice brown, letting them remain by the side of the fire after they are coloured, that the paste may be thoroughly done. Drain them before the fire, dish on a d'oyley, sprinkle over them sifted sugar, and serve. These cannelons are very delicious made with fresh instead of preserved fruit, such as strawberries, raspberries, or currants: it should be laid in the paste, plenty of pounded sugar sprinkled over, and folded and fried in the same manner as stated above. *Time.*—About 10 minutes. *Average cost*, 1s. *Sufficient.*—½ lb. of paste for a moderate-sized dish of cannelons. *Seasonable*, with jam, at any time.

CAPER SAUCE, for Fish.

Ingredients.—½ pint of melted butter, 3 dessertspoonfuls of capers, 1 dessertspoonful of their liquor, a small piece of glaze, if at hand (this may be dispensed with), ¼ teaspoonful of salt, ditto of pepper, 1 tablespoonful of anchovy essence. *Mode.*—Cut the capers across once or twice, but do not chop them fine; put them in a saucepan with ½ pint of good melted butter, and add all the other ingredients. Keep stirring the whole until it just simmers, when it is ready to serve. *Time.*—1 minute to simmer. *Average cost* for this quantity, 5d. *Sufficient* to serve with a skate, or 2 or 3 slices of salmon.

CAPER SAUCE, for Boiled Mutton.

Ingredients.—½ pint of melted butter, 3 tablespoonfuls of capers or nasturtiums, 1 tablespoonful of their liquor. *Mode.*—Chop the capers twice or thrice, and add them, with their liquor, to ½ pint of melted butter, made very smoothly with milk; keep stirring well; let the sauce just simmer, and serve in a tureen. Pickled nasturtium-pods are fine-flavoured, and by many are eaten in preference to capers. They make an excellent sauce. *Time.*—2 minutes to simmer. *Average cost* for this quantity, 8d. *Sufficient* to serve with a leg of mutton.

CAPER SAUCE, a Substitute for.

Ingredients.—½ pint of melted butter, 2 tablespoonfuls of cut parsley, ½ teaspoonful of salt, 1 tablespoonful of vinegar. *Mode.*—Boil the parsley slowly to let it become a bad colour; cut, but do not chop it fine. Add it to ½ pint of smoothly-made melted butter, with salt and vinegar in the above proportions. Boil up and serve. *Time.*—2 minutes to simmer. *Average cost* for this quantity, 3*d*.

CAPSICUMS, Pickled.

Ingredients.—Vinegar, ¼ oz. of pounded mace, and ¼ oz. of grated nutmeg, to each quart; brine. *Mode.*—Gather the pods with the stalks on, before they turn red; slit them down the side with a small-pointed knife, and remove the seeds only; put them in a strong brine for 3 days, changing it every morning; then take them out, lay them on a cloth, with another one over them, until they are perfectly free from moisture. Boil sufficient vinegar to cover them, with mace and nutmeg in the above proportions; put the pods in a jar, pour over the vinegar when cold, and exclude them from the air by means of a wet bladder tied over.

CARP, Baked.

Ingredients.—1 carp, forcemeat, bread-crumbs, 1 oz. butter, ½ pint of stock (*see* STOCK), ½ pint of port wine, 6 anchovies, 2 onions sliced, 1 bay-leaf, a faggot of sweet herbs, flour to thicken, the juice of 1 lemon; cayenne and salt to taste; ½ teaspoonful of powdered sugar. *Mode.*—Stuff the carp with a delicate forcemeat, after thoroughly cleansing it, and sew it up, to prevent the stuffing from falling out. Rub it over with an egg, and sprinkle it with bread-crumbs, lay it in a deep earthen dish, and drop the butter, oiled, over the bread-crumbs. Add the stock, onions, bay-leaf, herbs, wine, and anchovies, and bake for 1 hour. Put 1 oz. of butter into a stewpan, melt it, and dredge in sufficient flour to dry it up; put in the strained liquor from the carp, stir frequently, and when it has boiled, add the lemon-juice and seasoning. Serve the carp on a dish garnished with parsley and cut lemon, and the sauce in a boat. *Time.*—1¼ hour. *Average cost.* Seldom bought. *Seasonable* from March to October. *Sufficient* for 1 or 2 persons.

CARP, Stewed.

Ingredients.—1 carp, salt, stock, 2 onions, 6 cloves, 12 peppercorns, 1 blade of mace, ¼ pint of port wine, the juice of ½ lemon, cayenne and salt to taste, a faggot of savoury herbs. *Mode.*—Scale the fish, clean it nicely, and, if very large, divide it; lay it in the stewpan, after having rubbed a little salt on it, and put in sufficient stock to cover it; add the herbs, onions and spices, and stew gently for 1 hour, or rather more, should it be very large. Dish up the fish with great care, strain the liquor, and add to it the port wine, lemon-juice, and cayenne; give one boil, pour it over the fish, and serve. *Time.*—1¼ hour. *Average cost.* Seldom bought. *Seasonable* from March to October. *Sufficient* for 1 or 2 persons.

Note.—This fish can be boiled plain, and served with parsley and butter. Chub and Char may be cooked in the same manner as the above, as also Dace and Roach.

CARROT JAM, to Imitate Apricot Preserve.

Ingredients.—Carrots; to every lb. of carrot pulp allow 1 lb. of pounded sugar, the grated rind of 1 lemon, the strained juice of 2, 6 chopped bitter almonds, 2 tablespoonfuls of brandy. *Mode.*—Select young carrots; wash and scrape them clean, cut them into round pieces, put them into a saucepan with sufficient water to cover them, and let them simmer, until perfectly soft; then beat them through a sieve. Weigh the pulp, and to every lb. allow the above ingredients. Put the pulp into a preserving-pan with the sugar, and let this boil for 5 minutes, stirring and skimming all the time. When cold, add the lemon-rind and juice, almonds and brandy; mix these well with the jam; then put it into pots, which must be well covered and kept in a dry place. The brandy may be omitted, but the preserve will then not keep: with the brandy it will remain good for months. *Time.*—About ¾ hour to boil the carrots; 5 minutes to simmer the pulp. *Average cost*, 1*s.* 2*d.* for 1 lb. of pulp, with the other ingredients in proportion. *Sufficient* to fill 3 pots. *Seasonable* from July to December.

CARROT PUDDING, Baked or Boiled.

Ingredients.—½ lb. of bread-crumbs, 4 oz. suet, ¼ lb. of stoned raisins, ¾ lb. of carrot, ¼ lb. of currants, 3 oz. of sugar, 3 eggs, milk, ¼ nutmeg. *Mode.*—Boil the carrots, until tender enough to mash to a pulp; add the remaining ingredients, and moisten with sufficient milk to make the pudding of the consistency of thick batter. If to be boiled, put the mixture into a buttered basin, tie it down with a cloth, and boil for 2½ hours: if to be baked, put it into a pie-dish, and bake for nearly an hour; turn it out of the dish, strew sifted sugar over it, and serve. *Time.*—2½ hours to boil; 1 hour to bake. *Average cost*, 1*s*. 2*d*. *Sufficient* for 5 or 6 persons. *Seasonable* from September to March.

CARROT SOUP.

Ingredients.—4 quarts of liquor in which a leg of mutton or beef has been boiled, a few beef-bones, 6 large carrots, 2 large onions, 1 turnip; seasoning of salt and pepper to taste; cayenne. *Mode.*—Put the liquor, bones, onions, turnip, pepper, and salt, into a stewpan, and simmer for 3 hours. Scrape and cut the carrots thin, strain the soup on them, and stew them till soft enough to pulp through a hair sieve or coarse cloth; then boil the pulp with the soup, which should be of the consistency of pea-soup. Add cayenne. Pulp only the red part of the carrot, and make this soup the day before it is wanted. *Time.*—4½ hours. *Average cost*, per quart, 1½*d*. *Seasonable* from October to March. *Sufficient* for 8 persons.

CARROT SOUP.

Ingredients.—2 lbs. of carrots, 3 oz. of butter, seasoning to taste of salt and cayenne, 2 quarts of stock or gravy soup. *Mode.*—Scrape and cut out all specks from the carrots, wash, and wipe them dry, and then reduce them into quarter-inch slices. Put the butter into a large stewpan, and when it is melted, add 2 lbs. of the sliced carrots, and let them stow gently for an hour without browning. Add to them the soup, and allow them to simmer till tender,—say for nearly an hour. Press them through a strainer with the soup, and add salt and cayenne if required. Boil the whole gently for 5 minutes, skim well, and serve as hot as possible. *Time.*—1¼ hour. *Average cost*, per quart, 1*s*. 1*d*.

CARROTS, Boiled.

Ingredients.—To each ½ gallon of water, allow one heaped tablespoonful of salt; carrots. *Mode.*—Cut off the green tops, wash and scrape the carrots, and should there be any black specks, remove them. If very large, cut them in halves, divide them lengthwise into four pieces, and put them into boiling water, salted in the above proportion; let them boil until tender, which may be ascertained by thrusting a fork into them: dish, and serve very hot. This vegetable is an indispensable accompaniment to boiled beef. When thus served, it is usually boiled with the beef; a few carrots are placed round the dish as a garnish, and the remainder sent to table in a vegetable-dish. Young carrots do not require nearly so much boiling, nor should they be divided: these make a nice addition to stewed veal, &c. *Time.*—Large carrots, 1¾ to 2¼ hours; young ones, about ½ hour. *Average cost*, 6*d.* to 8*d.* per bunch of 18. *Sufficient.*—4 large carrots for 5 or 6 persons. *Seasonable.*—Young carrots from April to July, old ones at any time.

CARROTS, to dress, in the German way.

Ingredients.—8 large carrots, 3 oz. of butter, salt to taste, a very little grated nutmeg, 1 tablespoonful of finely-minced parsley, 1 dessertspoonful of minced onion, rather more than 1 pint of weak stock or broth, 1 tablespoonful of flour. *Mode.*—Wash and scrape the carrots, and cut them into rings of about ¼ inch in thickness. Put the butter into a stewpan; when it is melted, lay in the carrots, with salt, nutmeg, parsley, and onion in the above proportions. Toss the stewpan over the fire for a few minutes, and when the carrots are well saturated with the butter, pour in the stock, and simmer gently until they are nearly tender. Then put into another stewpan a small piece of butter; dredge in about a tablespoonful of flour; stir this over the fire, and when of a nice brown colour, add the liquor that the carrots have been boiling in; let this just boil up, pour it over the carrots in the other stewpan, and let them finish simmering until quite tender. Serve very hot. This vegetable, dressed as above, is a favourite accompaniment to roast pork, sausages, &c., &c. *Time.*—About ¾ hour. *Average cost*, 6*d.* to 8*d.* per bunch of 18. *Sufficient* for 6 or 7 persons. *Seasonable.*—Young carrots from April to July, old ones at any time.

CARROTS, Sliced (Entremets, or to be served with the Second Course, as a Side-Dish).

Ingredients.—5 or 6 large carrots, a large lump of sugar, 1 pint of weak stock, 3 oz. of fresh butter, salt to taste. *Mode.*—Scrape and wash the carrots, cut them into slices of an equal size, and boil them in salt and water until half done; drain them well, put them into a stewpan with the sugar and stock, and let them boil over a brisk fire. When reduced to a glaze, add the fresh butter and a seasoning of salt; shake the stewpan about well, and when the butter is well mixed with the carrots, serve. There should be no sauce in the dish when it comes to table, but it should all adhere to the carrots. *Time.*—Altogether, ¾ hour. *Average cost*, 6*d.* to 8*d.* per bunch of 18. *Sufficient* for 1 dish. *Seasonable.*—Young carrots from April to July, old ones at any time.

CARROTS, Stewed.

Ingredients.—7 or 8 large carrots, 1 teacupful of broth, pepper and salt to taste, ½ teacupful of cream, thickening of butter and flour. *Mode.*—Scrape the carrots nicely; half-boil, and slice them into a stewpan; add the broth, pepper and salt, and cream; simmer till tender, and be careful the carrots are not broken. A few minutes before serving, mix a little flour with about 1 oz. of butter; thicken the gravy with this; let it just boil up, and serve. *Time.*—About ¾ hour to boil the carrots, about 20 minutes to cook them after they are sliced. *Average cost*, 6*d.* to 8*d.* per bunch of 18. *Sufficient* for 5 or 6 persons. *Seasonable.*—Young carrots from April to July, old ones at any time.

CAULIFLOWERS à la SAUCE BLANCHE (Entremets, or Side-dish, to be served with the Second Course).

Ingredients.—3 cauliflowers, ½ pint of sauce blanche, or French melted butter, 3 oz. of butter, salt and water. *Mode.*—Cleanse the cauliflowers as in the succeeding recipe, and cut the stalks off flat at the bottom; boil them until tender in salt and water, to which the above proportion of butter has been added, and be careful to take them up the moment they are done, or they will break, and the appearance of the dish will be spoiled. Drain them well, and dish them in the shape of a large cauliflower. Have ready ½ pint of sauce made by recipe, pour it over the flowers, and serve hot and quickly. *Time.*—Small cauliflowers, 12 to 15 minutes; large ones, 20 to 25 minutes, after the water boils. *Average cost*, large cauliflowers, in full season, 6*d.* each. *Sufficient*, 1 large cauliflower for 3 or 4 persons. *Seasonable* from the beginning of June to the end of September.

CAULIFLOWERS, Boiled.

Ingredients.—To each ½ gallon of water allow 1 heaped tablespoonful of salt. *Mode.*—Choose cauliflowers that are close and white; trim off the decayed outside leaves, and cut the stalk off flat at the bottom. Open the flower a little in places to remove the insects, which are generally found about the stalk, and let the cauliflowers lie in salt and water for an hour previous to dressing them, with their heads downwards: this will effectually draw out all the vermin. Then put them into fast-boiling water, with the addition of salt in the above proportion, and let them boil briskly over a good fire, keeping the saucepan uncovered, and the water well skimmed. When the cauliflowers are tender, take them up with a slice; let them drain, and, if large enough, place them upright in the dish. Serve with plain melted butter, a little of which may be poured over the flower. *Time.*—Small cauliflower 12 to 15 minutes, large one 20 to 25 minutes, after the water boils. *Average cost*, for large cauliflowers, 6*d.* each. *Sufficient.*—Allow 1 large cauliflower for 3 persons. *Seasonable* from the beginning of June to the end of September.

BOILED CAULIFLOWER.

CAULIFLOWERS, with Parmesan Cheese (Entremets, or Side-dish, to be served with the Second Course).

Ingredients.—2 or 3 cauliflowers, rather more than ½ pint of white sauce, 2 tablespoonfuls of grated Parmesan cheese, 2 oz. of fresh butter, 3 tablespoonfuls of bread-crumbs. *Mode.*—Cleanse and boil the cauliflowers by the preceding recipe, drain them, and dish them with the flowers standing upright. Have ready the above proportion of white sauce; pour sufficient of it over the cauliflowers just to cover the top; sprinkle over this some rasped Parmesan cheese and bread-crumbs, and drop on these the butter, which should be melted, but not oiled. Brown with a salamander, or before the fire, and pour round, but not over, the flowers the remainder of the sauce, with which should be mixed a small quantity of grated Parmesan cheese. *Time.*—Altogether, ½ hour. *Average cost,* for large cauliflowers, 6*d.* each. *Sufficient.*—3 small cauliflowers for 1 dish. *Seasonable* from the beginning of June to the end of September.

CAYENNE CHEESES.

Ingredients.—½ lb. of butter, ½ lb. of flour, ½ lb. of grated cheese, 1/6 teaspoonful of cayenne, 1/3 teaspoonful of salt; water. *Mode.*—Rub the butter in the flour; add the grated cheese, cayenne, and salt, and mix these ingredients well together. Moisten with sufficient water to make the whole into a paste; roll out, and cut into fingers about 4 inches in length. Bake them in a moderate oven a very light colour, and serve very hot. *Time.*—15 to 20 minutes. *Average cost,* 1*s.* 4*d. Sufficient* for 6 or 7 persons. *Seasonable* at any time.

CAYENNE VINEGAR, or Essence of Cayenne.

Ingredients.—½ oz. of cayenne pepper, ½ pint of strong spirit, or 1 pint of vinegar. *Mode.*—Put the vinegar, or spirit, into a bottle, with the above proportion of cayenne, and let it steep for a month, when strain off and bottle for use. This is excellent seasoning for soups or sauces, but must be used very sparingly.

CELERY.

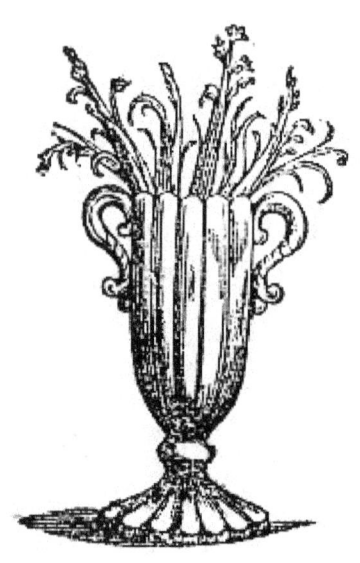

CELERY, IN GLASS.

With a good heart, and nicely blanched, this vegetable is generally eaten raw, and is usually served with the cheese. Let the roots be washed free from dirt, all the decayed and outside leaves being cut off, preserving as much of the stalk as possible, and all specks or blemishes being carefully removed. Should the celery be large, divide it lengthwise into quarters, and place it, root downwards, in a celery-glass, which should be rather more than half filled with water. The top leaves may be curled, by shredding them in narrow strips with the point of a clean skewer, at a distance of about 4 inches from the top. *Average cost,* 2*d.* per head. *Sufficient.*—Allow 2 heads for 4 or 5 persons. *Seasonable* from October to April.

Note.—This vegetable is exceedingly useful for flavouring soups, sauces, &c., and makes a very nice addition to winter salad.

CELERY SAUCE, for Boiled Turkey, Poultry, &c.

Ingredients.—6 heads of celery, 1 pint of white stock, 2 blades of mace, 1 small bunch of savoury herbs; thickening of butter and flour, or arrowroot, ½ pint of cream, lemon-juice. *Mode.*—Boil the celery in salt and water until tender, and cut it into pieces 2 inches long. Put the stock into a stewpan with the mace and herbs, and let it simmer for ½ hour to extract their flavour. Then strain the liquor, add the celery, and a thickening of butter kneaded with flour, or, what is still better, with arrowroot; just before serving, put in the cream, boil it up, and squeeze in a little lemon-juice. If necessary, add a seasoning of salt and white pepper. *Time.*—25 minutes to boil the celery. *Average cost*, 1*s*. 3*d*. *Sufficient*, this quantity for a boiled turkey.

Note.—This sauce may be made brown by using gravy instead of white stock, and flavouring it with mushroom ketchup or Harvey's sauce.

CELERY SAUCE (a more simple Recipe).

Ingredients.—4 heads of celery, ½ pint of melted butter made with milk, 1 blade of pounded mace; salt and white pepper to taste. *Mode.*—Wash the celery, boil it in salt and water till tender, and cut it into pieces 2 inches long; make ½ pint melted butter by recipe; put in the celery, pounded mace, and seasoning; simmer for 3 minutes, when the sauce will be ready to serve. *Time.*—25 minutes to boil the celery. *Average cost*, 6*d*. *Sufficient*, this quantity for a boiled fowl.

CELERY SOUP.

Ingredients.—9 heads of celery, 1 teaspoonful of salt, nutmeg to taste, 1 lump of sugar, ½ pint of strong stock, a pint of cream, and 2 quarts of boiling water. *Mode.*—Cut the celery into small pieces; throw it into the water, seasoned with the nutmeg, salt, and sugar. Boil it till sufficiently tender; pass it through a sieve, add the stock, and simmer it for half an hour. Now put in the cream, bring it to the boiling-point, and serve immediately. *Time.*—1 hour. *Average cost*, 1*s*. per quart. *Seasonable* from September to March. *Sufficient* for 8 persons.

Note.—This soup can be made brown instead of white, by omitting the cream, and colouring it a little. When celery cannot be procured, half a drachm of the seed, finely pounded, will give a flavour to the soup, if put in a quarter of an hour before it is done. A little of the essence of celery will answer the same purpose.

CELERY, Stewed, à la Crême.

Ingredients.—6 heads of celery; to each ½ gallon of water allow 1 heaped tablespoonful of salt, 1 blade of pounded mace, 1/3 pint of cream.

Mode.—Wash the celery thoroughly; trim, and boil it in salt and water until tender. Put the cream and pounded mace into a stewpan, shake it over the fire until the cream thickens, dish the celery, pour over the sauce, and serve. *Time.*—Large heads of celery, 25 minutes; small ones, 15 to 20 minutes. *Average cost*, 2d. per head. *Sufficient* for 5 or 6 persons. *Seasonable* from October to April.

CELERY, Stewed (with White Sauce).

Ingredients.—6 heads of celery, 1 oz. of butter; to each half gallon of water allow 1 heaped teaspoonful of salt, ½ pint of white sauce (*see* White Sauce). *Mode.*—Have ready sufficient boiling water just to cover the celery, with salt and butter in the above proportion. Wash the celery well, cut off the decayed outside leaves, trim away the green tops, and shape the root into a point; put it into the boiling water, let it boil rapidly until tender, then take it out, drain well, place it upon a dish, and pour over it about ½ pint of white sauce, made by recipe. It may also be plainly boiled as above, placed on toast, and melted butter poured over, the same as asparagus is dished. *Time.*—Large heads of celery 25 minutes, small ones 15 to 20 minutes, after the water boils. *Average cost*, 2d. per head. *Sufficient* for 5 or 6 persons. *Seasonable* from October to April.

CELERY, Stewed (with White Sauce).

Ingredients.—6 heads of celery, ½ pint of white stock or weak broth, 4 tablespoonfuls of cream, thickening of butter and flour, 1 blade of pounded mace, a *very little* grated nutmeg; pepper and salt to taste. *Mode.*—Wash the celery, strip off the outer leaves, and cut it into lengths of about 4 inches. Put these into a saucepan, with the broth, and stow till tender, which will be in from 20 to 25 minutes; then add the remaining ingredients, simmer altogether for 4 or 5 minutes, pour into a dish, and serve. It may be garnished with sippets of toasted bread. *Time.*—Altogether, ½ hour. *Average cost*, 2d. per head. *Sufficient* for 5 or 6 persons. *Seasonable* from October to April.

Note.—By cutting the celery into smaller pieces, by stewing it a little longer, and, when done, by pressing it through a sieve, the above stew may be converted into a Purée of Celery.

CELERY VINEGAR.

Ingredients.—¼ oz. of celery-seed, 1 pint of vinegar. *Mode.*—Crush the seed by pounding it in a mortar; boil the vinegar, and when cold, pour it to the seed; let it infuse for a fortnight, when strain and bottle off for use. This is frequently used in salads.

CHAMPAGNE-CUP.

Ingredients.—1 quart bottle of champagne, 2 bottles of soda-water, 1 liqueur-glass of brandy or Curaçoa, 2 tablespoonfuls of powdered sugar, 1 lb. of pounded ice, a sprig of green borage. *Mode.*—Put all the ingredients into a silver cup; stir them together, and serve the same as claret-cup. Should the above proportion of sugar not be found sufficient to suit some tastes, increase the quantity. When borage is not easily obtainable, substitute for it a few slices of cucumber-rind. *Seasonable.*—Suitable for pic-nics balls, weddings, and other festive occasions.

CHARLOTTE-AUX-POMMES.

Ingredients.—A few slices of rather stale bread ½ inch thick, clarified butter, apple marmalade, with about 2 dozen apples, ½ glass of sherry. *Mode.*—Cut a slice of bread the same shape as the bottom of a plain round mould, which has been well buttered, and a few strips the height of the mould, and about 1½ inch wide; dip the bread in clarified butter (or spread it with cold butter, if not wanted quite so rich); place the round piece at the bottom of the mould, and set the narrow strips up the sides of it, overlapping each other a little, that no juice from the apples may escape, and that they may hold firmly to the mould. Brush the *interior* over with the white of egg (this will assist to make the case firmer); fill it with the apple marmalade, with the addition of a little sherry, and cover them with a round piece of bread, also brushed over with egg, the same as the bottom; slightly press the bread down to make it adhere to the other pieces; put a plate on the top, and bake the *charlotte* in a brisk oven, of a light colour. Turn it out on the dish, strew sifted sugar over the top, and pour round it a little melted apricot jam. *Time.*—40 to 50 minutes. *Average cost*, 1*s*. 9*d*. *Sufficient* for 5 or 6 persons. *Seasonable* from July to March.

CHARLOTTE-AUX-POMMES.

CHARLOTTE-AUX-POMMES, an easy method of making.

Ingredients.—½ lb. of flour, ¼ lb. of butter, ¼ lb. of powdered sugar, ½ teaspoonful of baking-powder, 1 egg, milk, 1 glass of raisin-wine, apple marmalade, ¼ pint of cream, 2 dessert spoonfuls of pounded sugar, 2 tablespoonfuls of lemon-juice. *Mode.*—Make a cake with the flour, butter, sugar, and baking-powder; moisten with the egg and sufficient milk to make it the proper consistency, and bake it in a round tin. When cold, scoop out the middle, leaving a good thickness all round the sides, to prevent them breaking; take some of the scooped-out pieces, which should be trimmed into neat slices; lay them in the cake, and pour over sufficient raisin-wine, with the addition of a little brandy, if approved, to soak them well. Have ready some apple marmalade, made by recipe; place a layer of this over the soaked cake, then a layer of cake and a layer of apples; whip the cream to a froth, mixing with it the sugar and lemon-juice; pile it on the top of the *charlotte*, and garnish it with pieces of clear apple jelly. This dish is served cold, but may be eaten hot by omitting the cream, and merely garnishing the top with bright jelly just before it is sent to table. *Time.*—1 hour to bake the cake. *Average cost*, 2s. *Sufficient* for 5 or 6 persons. *Seasonable* from July to March.

CHARLOTTE, Russe (an elegant Sweet Entremets).

Ingredients.—About 18 Savoy biscuits, ¾ pint of cream, flavouring of vanilla, liqueurs, or wine, 1 tablespoonful of pounded sugar, ½ oz. of isinglass. *Mode.*—Procure about 18 Savoy biscuits, or ladies'-fingers, as they are sometimes called; brush the edges of them with the white of an egg, and line the bottom of a plain round mould, placing them like a star or rosette. Stand them upright all round the edge, carefully put them so closely together that the white of egg connects them firmly, and place this case in the oven for about 5 minutes, just to dry the egg. Whisk the cream to a stiff froth, with the sugar, flavouring, and melted isinglass; fill the charlotte with it, cover with a slice of sponge-cake cut in the shape of the mould; place it in ice, where let it remain till ready for table; then turn it on a dish, remove the mould, and serve. 1 tablespoonful of liqueur of any kind, or 4 tablespoonfuls of wine, would nicely flavour the above proportion of cream. For arranging the biscuits in the mould, cut them to the shape required, so that they fit in nicely, and level them with the mould at the top, that, when turned out, there may be something firm to rest upon. Great care and attention is required in the turning out of this dish, that the cream does not burst the case; and the edges of the biscuits must have the smallest quantity of egg brushed over them, or it would stick to the mould, and so prevent the charlotte from coming away properly. *Time.*—5 minutes in the oven. *Average cost,* with cream at 1*s.* per pint, 2*s.* 6*d. Sufficient* for 1 charlotte. *Seasonable* at any time.

CHEESE.

Cheese is the curd formed from milk by artificial coagulation, pressed and dried for use. Curd, called also casein and caseous matter, or the basis of cheese, exists in the milk, and not in the cream, and requires only to be separated by coagulation: the coagulation, however, supposes some alteration of the curd. By means of the substance employed to coagulate it, it is rendered insoluble in water. When the curd is freed from the whey, kneaded and pressed to expel it entirely, it becomes cheese; this assumes a degree of transparency, and possesses many of the properties of coagulated albumen. If it be well dried, it does not change by exposure to the air; but if it contain moisture, it soon putrefies; it therefore requires some salt to preserve it, and this acts likewise as a kind of seasoning. All our cheese is coloured more or less, except that made from skim milk. The colouring substances employed are arnatto, turmeric, or marigold, all perfectly harmless unless they are adulterated; and it is said that arnatto sometimes contains red lead.

Cheese varies in quality and richness according to the materials of which it is composed. It is made—1. Of entire milk, as in Cheshire; 2. of milk and cream, as at Stilton; 3. of new milk mixed with skim milk, as in Gloucestershire; 4. of skimmed milk only, as in Suffolk, Holland, and Italy.

The principal varieties of cheese used in England are the following: *Cheshire cheese,* famed all over Europe for its rich quality and fine piquante flavour. It is made of entire new milk, the cream not being taken off. *Gloucester cheese* is much milder in its taste than the Cheshire. There are two kinds of Gloucester cheese, single and double:—*Single Gloucester* is made of skimmed milk, or of the milk deprived of half the cream; *Double Gloucester* is a cheese that pleases almost every palate: it is made of the whole milk and cream. *Stilton cheese* is made by adding the cream of one day to the entire milk of the next: it was first made at Stilton, in Leicestershire. *Sage cheese* is so called from the practice of colouring some curd with bruised sage, marigold-leaves, and parsley, and mixing this with some uncoloured curd. With the Romans, and during the middle ages, this practice was extensively adopted. *Cheddar cheese* much resembles Parmesan. It has a very agreeable taste and flavour, and has a spongy appearance. *Brickbat cheese* has nothing remarkable except its form. It is made by turning with rennet a mixture of cream and new milk; the curd is put into a wooden vessel the shape of a brick, and is then pressed and dried in the usual way. *Dunlop cheese* has a peculiarly mild and rich taste: the best is made entirely from new milk. *New cheese* (as it is called in London) is made chiefly in Lincolnshire, and is either made of all cream, or, like Stilton, by adding the cream of one day's milking to the milk that comes immediately from the cow: they are extremely thin, and are compressed gently two or three times, turned for a few days, and then eaten new with radishes, salad, &c. *Skimmed Milk cheese* is made for sea voyages principally. *Parmesan cheese* is made in Parma and Piacenza. It is the most celebrated of all cheese: it is made entirely of skimmed cows' milk; the high flavour which it has is supposed to be owing to the rich herbage of the meadows of the Po, where the cows are pastured. The best Parmesan is kept for three or four years, and none is carried to market till it is at least six months old. *Dutch cheese* derives its peculiar pungent taste from the practice adopted in Holland of coagulating the milk with muriatic acid instead of rennet. *Swiss cheeses,* in their several varieties, are all remarkable for their fine flavour; that from *Gruyère,* a bailiwick in the canton of Fribourg, is best known in England; it is flavoured by the dried herb of *Melilotus officinalis* in powder. Cheese from milk and potatoes is manufactured in Thuringia and Saxony. *Cream cheese,* although so called, is not properly cheese, but is nothing more than cream dried sufficiently to be cut with a knife.

In families where much cheese is consumed, and it is bought in large quantities, a piece from the whole cheese should be cut, the larger quantity spread with a thickly-buttered sheet of white paper, and the outside occasionally wiped. To keep cheeses moist that are in daily use, when they come from table a damp cloth should be wrapped round them, and the cheese put into a pan with a cover to it, in a cool but not very dry place. To ripen cheeses, and bring them forward, put them into a damp cellar; and to check too large a production of mites, spirits may be poured into the parts affected. Pieces of cheese which are too near the rind, or too dry to put on table, may be made into Welsh rarebits, or grated down and mixed with macaroni. Cheeses may be preserved in a perfect state for years, by covering them with parchment made pliable by soaking in water, or by rubbing them over with a coating of melted fat. The cheeses selected should be free from cracks or bruises of any kind.

CHEESE-GLASS.

CHEESE, Mode of Serving.

The usual mode of serving cheese at good tables is to cut a small quantity of it into neat square pieces, and to put them into a glass cheese-dish, this dish being handed round. Should the cheese crumble much, of course this method is rather wasteful, and it may then be put on the table in the piece, and the host may cut from it. When served thus, the cheese must always be carefully scraped, and laid on a white d'oyley or napkin, neatly folded. Cream cheese is often served in a cheese course, and, sometimes, grated Parmesan: the latter should be put into a covered glass dish. Rusks, cheese-biscuits, pats or slices of butter, and salad, cucumber, or water-cresses, should always form part of a cheese-course.

CHEESE, Pounded.

Ingredients.—To every lb. of cheese allow 3 oz. of fresh butter. *Mode.*—To pound cheese is an economical way of using it if it has become dry; it is exceedingly good spread on bread, and is the best way of eating it for those whose digestion is weak. Cut up the cheese into small pieces, and pound it smoothly in a mortar, adding butter in the above proportion. Press it down into a jar, cover with clarified butter, and it will keep for several days. The flavour may be very much increased by adding mixed mustard (about a teaspoonful to every lb.), or cayenne, or pounded mace. Curry-powder is also not infrequently mixed with it.

CHEESE, Toasted, or Scotch Rarebit.

Ingredients.—A few slices of rich cheese, toast, mustard, and pepper. *Mode.*—Cut some nice rich sound cheese into rather thin slices; melt it in a cheese-toaster on a hot plate or over steam, and, when melted, add a small quantity of mixed mustard and a seasoning of pepper; stir the cheese until it is completely dissolved, then brown it before the fire, or with a salamander. Fill the bottom of the cheese-toaster with hot water, and serve with dry or buttered toasts, whichever may be preferred. Our engraving illustrates a cheese-toaster with hot-water reservoir: the cheese is melted in the upper tin, which is placed in another vessel of boiling water, so keeping the preparation beautifully hot. A small quantity of porter, or port wine, is sometimes mixed with the cheese; and, if it be not very rich, a few pieces of butter may be mixed with it to great advantage. Sometimes the melted cheese is spread on the toasts, and then laid in the cheese-dish at the top of the hot water. Whichever way it is served, it is highly necessary that the mixture be very hot, and very quickly sent to table, or it will be worthless. *Time.*—About 5 minutes to melt the cheese. *Average cost*, 1½d. per slice. *Sufficient.*—Allow a slice to each person. *Seasonable* at any time.

HOT-WATER CHEESE-DISH.

CHEESE, Toasted, or Welsh Rarebit.

Ingredients.—Slices of bread, butter, Cheshire or Gloucester cheese, mustard, and pepper. *Mode.*—Cut the bread into slices about ½ inch in thickness; pare off the crust, toast the bread slightly without hardening or burning it, and spread it with butter. Cut some slices, not quite so large as the bread, from a good rich fat cheese; lay them on the toasted bread in a cheese-toaster; be careful that the cheese does not burn, and let it be equally melted. Spread over the top a little made mustard and a seasoning of pepper, and serve very hot, with very hot plates. To facilitate the melting of the cheese, it may be cut into thin flakes, or toasted on one side before it is laid on the bread. As it is so essential to send this dish hot to table, it is a good plan to melt the cheese in small round silver or metal pans, and to send these pans to table, allowing one for each guest. Slices of dry or buttered toast should always accompany them, with mustard, pepper, and salt. *Time.*—About 5 minutes to melt the cheese. *Average cost*, 1½d. per slice. *Sufficient.*—Allow a slice to each person. *Seasonable* at any time.

Note.—Should the cheese be dry, a little butter mixed with it will be an improvement.

CHEESE SANDWICHES.

Ingredients.—Slices of brown bread-and-butter, thin slices of cheese. *Mode.*—Cut from a nice fat Cheshire, or any good rich cheese, some slices about ½ inch thick, and place them between some slices of brown bread-and-butter, like sandwiches. Place them on a plate in the oven, and, when the bread is toasted, serve on a napkin very hot and very quickly. *Time.*—10 minutes in a brisk oven. *Average cost*, 1½d. each sandwich. *Sufficient.*—Allow a sandwich for each person. *Seasonable* at any time.

CHEESECAKES.

Ingredients.—8 oz. of pressed curds, 2 oz. of ratafias, 6 oz. of sugar, 2 oz. of butter, the yolks of 6 eggs, nutmegs, salt, rind of 2 oranges or lemons. *Mode.*—Rub the sugar on the orange or lemon rind, and scrape it off. Press the curd in a napkin, to get rid of moisture; pound it thoroughly in a mortar with the other ingredients till the whole becomes a soft paste. Line 2 dozen, or more, tartlet-pans with good puff-paste, garnish these with the cheese-custard, place a strip of candied-peel on the top of each, and bake in a moderate oven a light colour; when done, shake a little sifted sugar over them. Currants, dried cherries, sultanas, and citron may be used instead of candied-peel. *Time.*—20 minutes to bake. *Average cost*, 6*d.* per dozen. *Seasonable* at any time.

CHEROKEE, or Store Sauce.

Ingredients.—½ oz. of cayenne pepper, 5 cloves of garlic, 2 tablespoonfuls of soy, 1 tablespoonful of walnut ketchup, 1 pint of vinegar. *Mode.*—Boil all the ingredients *gently* for about ½ hour; strain the liquor, and bottle off for use. *Time.*—½ hour. *Seasonable.*—This sauce can be made at any time.

CHERRIES, Dried.

Cherries may be put into a slow oven and thoroughly dried before they begin to change colour; they should then be taken out of the oven, tied in bunches, and stored away in a dry place. In the winter, they may be cooked with sugar for dessert, the same as Normandy pippins. Particular care must be taken that the oven be not too hot. Another method of drying cherries is to stone them, and to put them into a preserving-pan, with plenty of loaf sugar strewed amongst them. They should be simmered till the fruit shrivels, when they should be strained from the juice. The cherries should then be placed in an oven cool enough to dry without baking them. About 5 oz. of sugar would be required for 1 lb. of cherries, and the same syrup may be used again to do another quantity of fruit.

CHERRIES, Morello, to Preserve.

Ingredients.—To every lb. of cherries allow 1¼ lb. of sugar, 1 gill of water. *Mode.*—Select ripe cherries, pick off the stalks, and reject all that have any blemishes. Boil the sugar and water together for 5 minutes; put in the cherries, and boil them for 10 minutes, removing the scum as it rises. Then turn the fruit, &c., into a pan, and let it remain until the next day, when boil it all again for another 10 minutes, and, if necessary, skim well. Put the cherries into small pots, pour over them the syrup, and, when cold, cover down with oiled papers, and the tops of the jars with tissue-paper brushed over on both sides with the white of an egg, and keep in a dry place. *Time.*—Altogether, 25 minutes to boil. *Average cost,* from 8*d*. to 10*d*. per lb. pot. *Seasonable.*—Make this in July or August.

CHERRIES, to Preserve in Syrup (very delicious).

Ingredients.—4 lbs. of cherries, 3 lbs. of sugar, 1 pint of white-currant juice. *Mode.*—Let the cherries be as clear and as transparent as possible, and perfectly ripe; pick off the stalks, and remove the stones, damaging the fruit as little as you can. Make a syrup with the above proportion of sugar, mix the cherries with it, and boil them for about 15 minutes, carefully skimming them; turn them gently into a pan, and let them remain till the next day, then drain the cherries on a sieve, and put the syrup and white-currant juice into the preserving-pan again. Boil these together until the syrup is somewhat reduced and rather thick, then put in the cherries, and let them boil for about 5 minutes; take them off the fire, skim the syrup, put the cherries into small pots or wide-mouthed bottles; pour the syrup over, and, when quite cold, tie them down carefully, so that the air is quite excluded. *Time.*—15 minutes to boil the cherries in the syrup; 10 minutes to boil the syrup and currant-juice; 5 minutes to boil the cherries the second time. *Average cost* for this quantity, 3*s*. 6*d*. *Seasonable.*—Make this in July or August.

CHERRY BRANDY, to make.

Ingredients.—Morello cherries, good brandy; to every lb. of cherries allow 3 oz. of pounded sugar. *Mode.*—Have ready some glass bottles, which must be perfectly dry. Ascertain that the cherries are not too ripe and are freshly gathered, and cut off about half of the stalks. Put them into the bottles, with the above proportion of sugar to every lb. of fruit; strew this in between the cherries, and, when the bottles are nearly full, pour in sufficient brandy to reach just below the cork. A few peach or apricot kernels will add much to their flavour, or a few blanched bitter almonds. Put corks or bungs into the bottles, tie over them a piece of bladder, and store away in a dry place. The cherries will be fit to eat in 2 or 3 months, and will remain good for years. They are liable to shrivel and become tough if too much sugar be added to them. *Average cost*, 1*s*. to 1*s*. 6*d*. per lb. *Sufficient.*—1 lb. of cherries and about a ¼ pint of brandy for a quart bottle. *Seasonable* in August and September.

CHERRY JAM.

Ingredients.—To every lb. of fruit, weighed before stoning, allow ½ lb. of sugar; to every 6 lbs. of fruit allow 1 pint of red-currant juice, and to every pint of juice 1 lb. of sugar. *Mode.*—Weigh the fruit before stoning, and allow half the weight of sugar; stone the cherries, and boil them in a preserving-pan until nearly all the juice is dried up, then add the sugar, which should be crushed to powder, and the currant-juice, allowing 1 pint to every 6 lbs. of cherries (original weight), and 1 lb. of sugar to every pint of juice. Boil all together until it jellies, which will be in from 20 minutes to ½ hour; skim the jam well, keep it well stirred, and, a few minutes before it is done, crack some of the stones, and add the kernels: these impart a very delicious flavour to the jam. *Time.*—According to the quality of the cherries, from ¾ to 1 hour to boil them; 20 minutes to ½ hour with the sugar. *Average cost*, from 7*d.* to 8*d.* per lb. pot. *Sufficient.*—1 pint of fruit for a lb. pot of jam. *Seasonable.*—Make this in July or August.

CHERRY SAUCE, for Sweet Puddings (German Recipe).

Ingredients.—1 lb. of cherries, 1 tablespoonful of flour, 1 oz. of butter, ½ pint of water, 1 wineglassful of port wine, a little grated lemon-rind, 4 pounded cloves, 2 tablespoonfuls of lemon-juice, sugar to taste. *Mode.*—Stone the cherries, and pound the kernels in a mortar to a smooth paste; put the butter and flour into a saucepan, stir them over the fire until of a pale brown, then add the cherries, the pounded kernels, the wine, and the water. Simmer these gently for ¼ hour, or until the cherries are quite cooked, and rub the whole through a hair sieve; add the remaining ingredients, let the sauce boil for another 5 minutes, and serve. This is a delicious sauce to serve with boiled batter pudding, and when thus used, should be sent to table poured over the pudding. *Time.*—20 minutes to ½ hour. *Average cost*, 1*s.* 2*d. Sufficient* for 4 or 5 persons. *Seasonable* in June, July, and August.

CHERRY TART.

Ingredients.—1½ lb. of cherries, 2 small tablespoonfuls of moist sugar, ½ lb. of short crust. *Mode.*—Pick the stalks from the cherries, put them, with the sugar, into a *deep* pie-dish just capable of holding them, with a small cup placed upside down in the midst of them. Make a short crust with ½ lb. of flour, by either of the recipes for short crust, lay a border round the edge of the dish, put on the cover, and ornament the edges; bake in a brisk oven from ½ hour to 40 minutes; strew finely-sifted sugar over, and serve hot or cold, although the latter is the more usual mode. It is more economical to make two or three tarts at one time, as the trimmings from one tart answer for lining the edges of the dish for another, and so much paste is not required as when they are made singly. Unless for family use, never make fruit pies in very *large* dishes; select them, however, as *deep* as possible. *Time.*—½ hour to 40 minutes. *Average cost*, in full season, 8*d*. *Sufficient* for 5 or 6 persons. *Seasonable* in June, July, and August.

Note.—A few currants added to the cherries will be found to impart a nice piquante taste to them.

CHESTNUT SAUCE, Brown.

Ingredients.—½ lb. of chestnuts, ½ pint of stock, 2 lumps of sugar, 4 tablespoonfuls of Spanish sauce (*see* Sauces). *Mode.*—Prepare the chestnuts as in the succeeding recipe, by scalding and peeling them; put them in a stewpan with the stock and sugar, and simmer them till tender. When done, add Spanish sauce in the above proportion, and rub the whole through a tammy. Keep this sauce rather liquid, as it is liable to thicken. *Time.*—1½ hour to simmer the chestnuts. *Average cost*, 8*d*.

CHESTNUT SAUCE, for Fowls or Turkey.

Ingredients.—½ lb. of chestnuts, ½ pint of white stock, 2 strips of lemon-peel, cayenne to taste, ¼ pint of cream or milk. *Mode.*—Peel off the outside skin of the chestnuts, and put them into boiling water for a few minutes; take off the thin inside peel, and put them into a saucepan with the white stock and lemon-peel, and let them simmer for 1½ hour, or until the chestnuts are quite tender. Rub the whole through a hair-sieve with a wooden spoon; add seasoning and the cream; let it just simmer, but not boil, and keep stirring all the time. Serve very hot, and quickly. If milk is used instead of cream, a very small quantity of thickening may be required: that, of course, the cook will determine. *Time.*—Altogether, nearly 2 hours. *Average cost*, 8*d*. *Sufficient*, this quantity for a turkey.

CHESTNUT (Spanish) SOUP.

Ingredients.—¾ lb. of Spanish chestnuts, ¼ pint of cream; seasoning to taste of salt, cayenne, and mace; 1 quart of stock. *Mode.*—Take the outer rind from the chestnuts, and put them into a large pan of warm water. As soon as this becomes too hot for the fingers to remain in it, take out the chestnuts, peel them quickly, and immerse them in cold water, and wipe and weigh them. Now cover them with good stock, and stew them gently for rather more than ¾ of an hour, or until they break when touched with a fork; then drain, pound, and rub them through a fine sieve reversed; add sufficient stock, mace, cayenne, and salt, and stir it often until it boils, and put in the cream. The stock in which the chestnuts are boiled can be used for the soup, when its sweetness is not objected to, or it may, in part, be added to it; and the rule is, that ¾ lb. of chestnuts should be given to each quart of soup. *Time.*—Rather more than 1 hour. *Average cost*, per quart, 1*s.* 6*d*. *Sufficient* for 4 persons. *Seasonable* from October to February.

CHICKENS, Boiled.

BOILED FOWL.

Ingredients.—A pair of chickens, water. *Choosing and Trussing.*—In choosing fowls for boiling, it should be borne in mind that those which are not black-legged are generally much whiter when dressed. Pick, draw, singe, wash, and truss them in the following manner, without the livers in the wings; and, in drawing, be careful not to break the gall-bladder:—Cut off the neck, leaving sufficient skin to skewer back. Cut the feet off to the first joint, tuck the stumps into a slit made on each side of the belly, twist the wings over the back of the fowl, and secure the top of the leg and the bottom of the wing together by running a skewer through them and the body. The other side must be done in the same manner. Should the fowl be very large and old, draw the sinews of the legs before tucking them in. Make a slit in the apron of the fowl, large enough to admit the parson's nose, and tie a string on the tops of the legs to keep them in their proper place. *Mode.*—When they are firmly trussed, put them into a stewpan with plenty of hot water, bring it to boil, and carefully remove all the scum as it rises. *Simmer very gently* until the fowl is tender, and bear in mind that the slower it boils the plumper and whiter will the fowl be. Many cooks wrap them in a floured cloth to preserve the colour, and to prevent the scum from clinging to them; in this case, a few slices of lemon should be placed on the breasts, over these a sheet of buttered paper, and then the cloth; cooking them in this manner renders the flesh very white. Boiled ham, bacon, boiled tongue, or pickled pork, are the usual accompaniments to boiled fowls, and they may be served with Béchamel, white sauce, parsley and butter, oyster, lemon, liver, celery, or mushroom sauce. A little should be poured over the fowls after the skewers are removed, and the remainder sent in a tureen to table. *Time.*—Large fowl, 1 hour; moderate-sized one, ¾ hour; chicken, from 20 minutes to ½ hour. *Average cost*, in full season, 5*s*. the pair. *Sufficient* for 7 or 8 persons. *Seasonable* all the year, but scarce in early spring.

CHICKEN BROTH.

Ingredients.—½ fowl, or the inferior joints of a whole one; 1 quart of water, 1 blade of mace, ½ onion, a small bunch of sweet herbs, salt to taste, 10 peppercorns. *Mode.*—An old fowl not suitable for eating may be converted into very good broth; or, if a young one be used, the inferior joints may be put in the broth, and the best pieces reserved for dressing in some other manner. Put the fowl into a saucepan, stew all the ingredients, and simmer gently for 1½ hour, carefully skimming the broth well. When done, strain, and put by in a cool place until wanted; then take all the fat off the top, warm up as much as may be required, and serve. This broth is, of course, only for those invalids whose stomachs are strong enough to digest it, with a flavouring of herbs, &c. It may be made in the same manner as beef tea, with water and salt only, but the preparation will be but tasteless and insipid. When the invalid cannot digest this chicken broth with the flavouring, we would recommend plain beef tea in preference to plain chicken tea, which it would be without the addition of herbs, onions, &c. *Time.*—1½ hour. *Sufficient* to make rather more than 1 pint of broth.

CHICKEN, Curried.

[Cold Meat Cookery.] *Ingredients.*—The remains of cold roast fowls, 2 large onions, 1 apple, 2 oz. of butter, 1 dessertspoonful of curry-powder, 1 teaspoonful of flour, ½ pint of gravy, 1 tablespoonful of lemon-juice. *Mode.* —Slice the onions, peel, core, and chop the apple, and cut the fowl into neat joints; fry these in the butter of a nice brown, then add the curry-powder, flour, and gravy, and stew for about 20 minutes. Put in the lemon-juice, and serve with boiled rice, either placed in a ridge round the dish or separately. Two or three shalots or a little garlic may be added, if approved. *Time.*— Altogether, ½ hour. *Average cost*, exclusive of the cold fowl, 6*d*. *Seasonable* in the winter.

CHICKEN CUTLETS (an Entrée).

Ingredients.—2 chickens; seasoning to taste of salt, white pepper, and cayenne; 2 blades of pounded mace, egg and bread-crumbs, clarified butter, 1 strip of lemon-rind, 2 carrots, 1 onion, 2 tablespoonfuls of mushroom ketchup, thickening of butter and flour, 1 egg. *Mode.*—Remove the breast and leg-bones of the chickens; cut the meat into neat pieces after having skinned it, and season the cutlets with pepper, salt, pounded mace, and cayenne. Put the bones, trimmings, &c., into a stewpan with 1 pint of water, adding carrots, onions, and lemon-peel in the above proportion; stew gently for 1½ hour, and strain the gravy. Thicken it with butter and flour, add the ketchup and 1 egg well beaten; stir it over the fire, and bring it to the simmering-point, but do not allow it to boil. In the mean time, egg and bread-crumb the cutlets, and give them a few drops of clarified butter; fry them a delicate brown, occasionally turning them; arrange them pyramidically on the dish, and pour over them the sauce. *Time.*—10 minutes to fry the cutlets. *Average cost*, 2*s*. each. *Sufficient* for an entrée. *Seasonable* from April to July.

CHICKEN CUTLETS, French.

[COLD MEAT COOKERY.] *Ingredients.*—The remains of cold roast or boiled fowl, fried bread, clarified butter, the yolk of 1 egg, bread-crumbs, ½ teaspoonful of finely-minced lemon-peel; salt, cayenne, and mace to taste. For sauce,—1 oz. of butter, 2 minced shalots, a few slices of carrot, a small bunch of savoury herbs, including parsley, 1 blade of pounded mace, 6 peppercorns, ½ pint of gravy. *Mode.*—Cut the fowls into as many nice cutlets as possible; take a corresponding number of sippets about the same size, all cut one shape; fry them a pale brown, put them before the fire, then dip the cutlets into clarified butter mixed with the yolk of an egg, cover with bread-crumbs seasoned in the above proportion, with lemon-peel, mace, salt, and cayenne; fry them for about 5 minutes, put each piece on one of the sippets, pile them high in the dish, and serve with the following sauce, which should be made ready for the cutlets. Put the butter into a stewpan, add the shalots, carrot, herbs, mace, and peppercorns; fry for 10 minutes, or rather longer; pour in ½ pint of good gravy, made of the chicken-bones; stew gently for 20 minutes, strain it, and serve. *Time.*—5 minutes to fry the cutlets; 35 minutes to make the gravy. *Average cost*, exclusive of the chicken, 9*d*. *Seasonable* from April to July.

CHICKEN, Fricasseed (an Entrée).

Ingredients.—2 small fowls or 1 large one, 3 oz. of butter, a bunch of parsley and green onions, 1 clove, 2 blades of mace, 1 shalot, 1 bay-leaf, salt and white pepper to taste, ¼ pint of cream, the yolks of 3 eggs. *Mode.*—Choose a couple of fat plump chickens, and, after drawing, singeing, and washing them, skin, and carve them into joints; blanch these in boiling water for 2 or 3 minutes, take them out, and immerse them in cold water to render them white. Put the trimmings, with the necks and legs, into a stewpan; add the parsley, onions, clove, mace, shalot, bay-leaf, and a seasoning of pepper and salt; pour to these the water that the chickens were blanched in, and simmer gently for rather more than 1 hour. Have ready another stewpan; put in the joints of fowl, with the above proportion of butter; dredge them with flour, let them get hot, but do not brown them much; then moisten the fricassee with the gravy made from the trimmings, &c., and stew very gently for ½ hour. Lift the fowl into another stewpan, skim the sauce, reduce it quickly over the fire by letting it boil fast, and strain it over them. Add the cream, and a seasoning of pounded mace and cayenne; let it boil up, and when ready to serve, stir to it the well-beaten yolks of 3 eggs; these should not be put in till the last moment, and the sauce should be made *hot*, but must *not boil*, or it will instantly curdle. A few button-mushrooms stewed with the fowl are by many persons considered an improvement. *Time.*—1 hour to make the gravy, ½ hour to simmer the fowl. *Average cost*, 5*s.* the pair. *Sufficient.*—1 large fowl for 1 entrée. *Seasonable* at any time.

CHICKEN (or Fowl) PATTIES.

[Cold Meat Cookery.] *Ingredients.*—The remains of cold roast chicken or fowl; to every ¼ lb. of meat allow 2 oz. of ham, 3 tablespoonfuls of cream, 2 tablespoonfuls of veal gravy, ½ teaspoonful of minced lemon-peel; cayenne, salt, and pepper to taste; 1 tablespoonful of lemon-juice, 1 oz. of butter rolled in flour, puff paste. *Mode.*—Mince very small the white meat from a cold roast fowl, after removing all the skin; weigh it, and to every ¼ lb. of meat allow the above proportion of minced ham. Put these into a stewpan with the remaining ingredients, stir over the fire for 10 minutes or ¼ hour, taking care that the mixture does not burn. Roll out some puff paste about ¼ inch in thickness, line the patty-pans with this, put upon each a small piece of bread, and cover with another layer of paste; brush over with the yolk of an egg, and bake in a brisk oven for about ¼ hour. When done, cut a round piece out of the top, and, with a small spoon, take out the bread (be particular in not breaking the outside border of the crust), and fill the patties with the mixture. *Time.*—¼ hour to prepare the meat; not quite ¼ hour to bake the crust. *Seasonable* at any time.

CHICKEN (or Fowl) PIE.

Ingredients.—2 small fowls or 1 large one, white pepper and salt to taste, ½ teaspoonful of grated nutmeg, ½ teaspoonful of pounded mace, forcemeat, a few slices of ham, 3 hard-boiled eggs, ½ pint of water, puff crust. *Mode.*—Skin and cut up the fowls into joints, and put the neck, leg, and backbones in a stewpan, with a little water, an onion, a bunch of savoury herbs, and a blade of mace; let these stew for about an hour, and, when done, strain off the liquor: this is for gravy, Put a layer of fowl at the bottom of a pie-dish, then a layer of ham, then one of forcemeat and hard-boiled eggs cut in rings; between the layers put a seasoning of pounded mace, nutmeg, pepper, and salt. Proceed in this manner until the dish is full, and pour in about ½ pint of water; border the edge of the dish with puff crust, put on the cover, ornament the top, and glaze it by brushing over it the yolk of an egg. Bake from 1¼ to 1½ hour, should the pie be very large, and, when done, pour in at the top the gravy made from the bones. If to be eaten cold, and wished particularly nice, the joints of the fowls should be boned, and placed in the dish with alternate layers of forcemeat; sausage-meat may also be substituted for the forcemeat, and is now very much used. When the chickens are boned, and mixed with sausage-meat, the pie will take about 2 hours to bake. It should be covered with a piece of paper when about half-done, to prevent the paste being dried up or scorched. *Time.*—For a pie with unboned meat, 1¼ to 1½ hour; with boned meat and sausage or forcemeat, 1½ to 2 hours. *Average cost*, with 2 fowls, 6*s*. 6*d*. *Sufficient* for 6 or 7 persons. *Seasonable* at any time.

CHICKEN, Potted (a Luncheon or Breakfast Dish).

Ingredients.—The remains of cold roast chicken; to every lb. of meat allow ¼ lb. of fresh butter, salt and cayenne to taste, 1 teaspoonful of pounded mace, ½ small nutmeg. *Mode.*—Strip the meat from the bones of cold roast fowl; when it is freed from gristle and skin, weigh it, and to every lb. of meat allow the above proportion of butter, seasoning, and spices. Cut the meat into small pieces, pound it well with the fresh butter, sprinkle in the spices gradually, and keep pounding until reduced to a perfectly smooth paste. Put it into potting-pots for use, and cover it with clarified butter, about ¼ inch in thickness, and, if to be kept for some time, tie over a bladder: 2 or 3 slices of ham, minced and pounded with the above ingredients, will be found an improvement. It should be kept in a dry place. *Seasonable* at any time.

CHICKEN (or Fowl) SALAD.

Ingredients.—The remains of cold roast or boiled chicken, 2 lettuces, a little endive, 1 cucumber, a few slices of boiled beetroot, salad-dressing. *Mode.*—Trim neatly the remains of the chicken; wash, dry, and slice the lettuces, and place in the middle of a dish; put the pieces of fowl on the top, and pour the salad-dressing over them. Garnish the edge of the salad with hard-boiled eggs cut in rings, sliced cucumber, and boiled beetroot cut in slices. Instead of cutting the eggs in rings, the yolks may be rubbed through a hair sieve, and the whites chopped very finely, and arranged on the salad in small bunches, yellow and white alternately. This should not be made long before it is wanted for table. *Average cost*, exclusive of the cold chicken, 8*d*. *Sufficient* for 4 or 5 persons. *Seasonable* at any time.

CHILI VINEGAR.

Ingredients.—50 fresh red English chilies, 1 pint of vinegar. *Mode*.—Pound or cut the chilies in half, and infuse them in the vinegar for a fortnight, when it will be fit for use. This will be found an agreeable relish to fish, as many people cannot eat it without the addition of an acid and cayenne pepper.

CHINA CHILO.

Ingredients.—1½ lb. of leg, loin, or neck of mutton, 2 onions, 2 lettuces, 1 pint of green peas, 1 teaspoonful of salt, 1 teaspoonful of pepper, ¼ pint of water, ¼ lb. of clarified butter; when liked, a little cayenne. *Mode*.—Mince the above quantity of undressed leg, loin, or neck of mutton, adding a little of the fat, also minced; put it into a stewpan with the remaining ingredients, previously shredding the lettuce and onion rather fine; closely cover the stewpan, after the ingredients have been well stirred, and simmer gently for rather more than two hours. Serve in a dish, with a border of rice round, the same as for curry. *Time*.—Rather more than two hours. *Average cost*, 1*s*. 6*d*. *Sufficient* for 3 or 4 persons. *Seasonable* from June to August.

MILL.

CHOCOLATE, to Make.

Ingredients.—Allow ½ oz. of chocolate to each person; to every oz. allow ½ pint of water, ½ pint of milk. *Mode.*—Make the milk-and-water hot; scrape the chocolate into it, and stir the mixture constantly and quickly until the chocolate is dissolved; bring it to the boiling-point, stir it well, and serve directly with white sugar. Chocolate prepared within a mill, as shown in the engraving, is made by putting in the scraped chocolate, pouring over it the boiling milk-and-water, and milling it over the fire until hot and frothy. *Sufficient.*—Allow ½ oz. of cake chocolate to each person.

CHOCOLATE CREAM.

Ingredients.—3 oz. of grated chocolate, ¼ lb. of sugar, 1½ pint of cream, 1½ oz. of clarified isinglass, the yolks of 6 eggs. *Mode.*—Beat the yolks of the eggs well, put them into a basin with the grated chocolate, the sugar, and 1 pint of the cream; stir these ingredients well together, pour them into a jug, and set this jug in a saucepan of boiling water; stir it one way until the mixture thickens, but *do not allow it to boil*, or it will curdle. Strain the cream through a sieve into a basin; stir in the isinglass and the other ½ pint of cream, which should be well whipped; mix all well together, and pour it into a mould which has been previously oiled with the purest salad-oil, and, if at hand, set it in ice until wanted for table. *Time.*—About 10 minutes to stir the mixture over the fire. *Average cost*, 4s. 6d., with cream at 1s. per pint. *Sufficient* to fill a quart mould. *Seasonable* at any time.

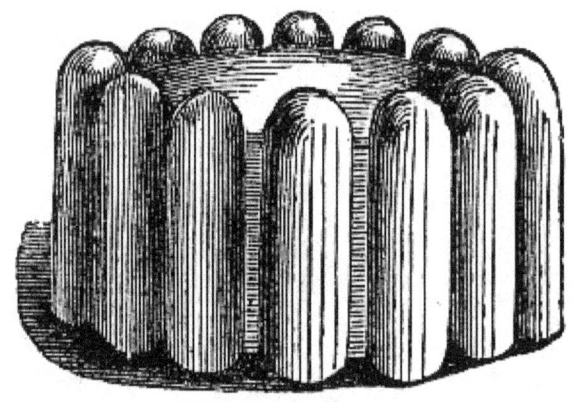

CREAM-MOULD.

CHOCOLATE SOUFFLÉ.

Ingredients.—4 eggs, 3 teaspoonfuls of pounded sugar, 1 teaspoonful of flour, 3 oz. of the best chocolate. *Mode.*—Break the eggs, separating the whites from the yolks, and put them into different basins; add to the yolks the sugar, flour, and chocolate, which should be very finely grated, and stir these ingredients for 5 minutes. Then well whisk the whites of the eggs in the other basin until they are stiff, and, when firm, mix lightly with the yolks till the whole forms a smooth and light substance; butter a round cake-tin, put in the mixture, and bake in a moderate oven from 15 to 20 minutes. Pin a white napkin round the tin, strew sifted sugar over the top of the soufflé, and send it immediately to table. The proper appearance of this dish depends entirely on the expedition with which it is served; and some cooks, to preserve its lightness, hold a salamander over the soufflé until it is placed on the table. If allowed to stand after it comes from the oven it will be entirely spoiled, as it falls almost immediately. *Time.*—15 to 20 minutes. *Average cost*, 1s. *Sufficient* for a moderate-sized soufflé. *Seasonable* at any time.

CLARET-CUP.

CLARET-CUP.

Ingredients.—1 bottle of claret, 1 bottle of soda-water, about ½ lb. of pounded ice, 4 tablespoonfuls of powdered sugar, ¼ teaspoonful of grated nutmeg, 1 liqueur-glass of Maraschino, a sprig of green borage. *Mode.*—Put all the ingredients into a silver cup, regulating the proportion of ice by the state of the weather; if very warm, a larger quantity would be necessary. Hand the cup round with a clean napkin passed through one of the handles, that the edge of the cup may be wiped after each guest has partaken of the contents thereof. *Seasonable* in summer.

COCK-A-LEEKIE.

Ingredients.—A capon or large fowl (sometimes an old cock, from which the recipe takes its name, is used), which should be trussed as for boiling, 2 or 3 bunches of fine leeks, 5 quarts of stock (*see* S<small>TOCK</small>), pepper and salt to taste. *Mode.*—Well wash the leeks (and, if old, scald them in boiling water for a few minutes), taking off the roots and part of the heads, and cut them into lengths of about an inch. Put the fowl into the stock, with, at first, one half of the leeks, and allow it to simmer gently. In half an hour add the remaining leeks, and then it may simmer for 3 or 4 hours longer. It should be carefully skimmed, and can be seasoned to taste. In serving, take out the fowl and carve it neatly, placing the pieces in a tureen, and pouring over them the soup, which should be very thick of leeks (a *purée* of leeks, the French would call it). *Time.*—4 hours. *Average cost*, 1*s*. 6*d*. per quart; or with stock, 1*s*. *Sufficient* for 10 persons. *Seasonable* in winter.

Note.—Without the fowl, the above, which would then be merely called leek soup, is very good, and also economical. Cock-a-leekie was largely consumed at the Burns Centenary Festival at the Crystal Palace, Sydenham, in 1859.

COCOA, to Make.

Ingredients.—Allow 2 teaspoonfuls of the prepared cocoa to 1 breakfast-cup; boiling milk and boiling water. *Mode.*—Put the cocoa into a breakfast-cup, pour over it sufficient cold milk to make it into a smooth paste; then add equal quantities of boiling milk and boiling water, and stir all well together. Care must be taken not to allow the milk to get burnt, as it will entirely spoil the flavour of the preparation. The above directions are usually given for making the prepared cocoa. The rock cocoa, or that bought in a solid piece, should be scraped, and made in the same manner, taking care to rub down all the lumps before the boiling liquid is added. *Sufficient.*—2 teaspoonfuls of prepared cocoa for 1 breakfast-cup, or ¼ oz. of the rock cocoa for the same quantity.

COD.

Cod should be chosen for the table when it is plump and round near the tail, when the hollow behind the head is deep, and when the sides are undulated as if they were ribbed. The glutinous parts about the head lose their delicate flavour after the fish has been twenty-four hours out of the water. The great point by which the cod should be judged is the firmness of its flesh; and, although the cod is not firm when it is alive, its quality may be arrived at by pressing the finger into the flesh: if this rises immediately, the flesh is good; if not, it is stale. Another sign of its goodness is, if the fish, when it is cut, exhibits a bronze appearance, like the silver side of a round of beef; when this is the case the flesh will be firm when cooked. Stiffness in a cod, or in any other fish, is a sure sign of freshness, though not always of quality. Sometimes codfish, though exhibiting signs of rough usage, will eat much better than those with red gills, so strongly recommended by many cookery-books. This appearance is generally caused by the fish having been knocked about at sea, in the well-boats, in which they are conveyed from the fishing-grounds to market.

COD à la BÉCHAMEL.

[COLD MEAT COOKERY.] *Ingredients.*—Any remains of cold cod, 4 tablespoonfuls of béchamel (*see* BÉCHAMEL SAUCE), 2 oz. of butter; seasoning to taste of pepper and salt; fried bread, a few bread-crumbs. *Mode.*—Flake the cod carefully, leaving out all skin and bone; put the béchamel in a stewpan with the butter, and stir it over the fire till the latter is melted; add seasoning, put in the fish, and mix it well with the sauce. Make a border of fried bread round the dish, lay in the fish, sprinkle over with bread-crumbs, and baste with butter. Brown either before the fire or with a salamander, and garnish with toasted bread cut in fanciful shapes. *Time.*—½ hour. *Average cost*, exclusive of the fish, 6*d.*

COD à la CREME.

[COLD MEAT COOKERY.] *Ingredients.*—1 large slice of cod, 1 oz. of butter, 1 chopped shalot, a little minced parsley, ¼ teacupful of white stock, ¼ pint of milk or cream, flour to thicken, cayenne and lemon-juice to taste, ¼ teaspoonful of powdered sugar. *Mode.*—Boil the cod, and while hot, break it into flakes; put the butter, shalot, parsley, and stock into a stewpan, and let them boil for 5 minutes. Stir in sufficient flour to thicken, and pour to it the milk or cream. Simmer for 10 minutes, add the cayenne and sugar, and, when liked, a little lemon-juice. Put the fish in the sauce to warm gradually, but do not let it boil. Serve in a dish garnished with croûtons. *Time.*—Rather more than ½ hour. *Average cost*, with cream, 2*s. Sufficient* for 3 persons. *Seasonable* from November to March.

Note.—The remains of fish from the preceding day answer very well for this dish.

COD à l'ITALIENNE.

Ingredients.—2 slices of crimped cod, 1 shalot, 1 slice of ham minced very fine, ½ pint of white stock, when liked, ½ teacupful of cream; salt to taste; a few drops of garlic vinegar, a little lemon-juice, ½ teaspoonful of powdered sugar. *Mode.*—Chop the shalots, mince the ham very fine, pour on the stock, and simmer for 15 minutes. If the colour should not be good, add cream in the above proportion, and strain it through a fine sieve; season it, and put in the vinegar, lemon-juice, and sugar. Now boil the cod, take out the middle bone, and skin it; put it on the dish without breaking, and pour the sauce over it. *Time.*—¾ hour. *Average cost*, 3s. 6d., with fresh fish. *Sufficient* for 4 persons. *Seasonable* from November to March.

COD à la MAÎTRE D'HÔTEL.

[COLD MEAT COOKERY.] *Ingredients.*—2 slices of cod, ¼ lb. of butter, a little chopped shalot and parsley; pepper to taste; ¼ teaspoonful of grated nutmeg, or rather less when the flavour is not liked; the juice of ¼ lemon. *Mode.*—Boil the cod, and either leave it whole, or, what is still better, flake it from the bone, and take off the skin. Put it into a stewpan with the butter, parsley, shalot, pepper, and nutmeg. Melt the butter gradually, and be very careful that it does not become like oil. When all is well mixed and thoroughly hot, add the lemon-juice, and serve. *Time.*—½ hour. *Average cost*, 2s. 6d.; with remains of cold fish, 5d. *Sufficient* for 4 persons. *Seasonable* from November to March.

Note.—Cod that has been left will do for this.

COD, Curried.

[COLD MEAT COOKERY.] *Ingredients.*—2 slices of large cod, or the remains of any cold fish; 3 oz. of butter, 1 onion sliced, a teacupful of white stock, thickening of butter and flour, 1 *small* teaspoonful of curry-powder, ¼ pint of cream, salt and cayenne to taste. *Mode.*—Flake the fish, and fry it of a nice brown colour with the butter and onions; put this in a stewpan, add the stock and thickening, and simmer for 10 minutes. Stir the curry-powder into the cream; put it, with the seasoning, to the other ingredients; give one boil, and serve. *Time.*—¾ hour. *Average cost*, with fresh fish, 3s. *Sufficient* for 4 persons. *Seasonable* from November to March.

COD PIE.

Ingredients.—2 slices of cod; pepper and salt to taste; ½ a teaspoonful of grated nutmeg, 1 large blade of pounded mace, 2 oz. of butter, ½ pint of stock, a paste crust (*see* PASTRY). For sauce,—1 tablespoonful of stock, ¼ pint of cream or milk, thickening of flour or butter, lemon-peel chopped very fine to taste, 12 oysters. *Mode.*—Lay the cod in salt for 4 hours, then wash it and place it in a dish; season, and add the butter and stock; cover with the crust, and bake for 1 hour, or rather more. Now make the sauce, by mixing the ingredients named above; give it one boil, and pour it into the pie by a hole made at the top of the crust, which can easily be covered by a small piece of pastry cut and baked in any fanciful shape,—such as a leaf, or otherwise. *Time.*—1½ hour. *Average cost*, with fresh fish, 2*s.* 6*d.* *Sufficient* for 6 persons. *Seasonable* from November to March.

Note.—The remains of cold fish may be used for this pie.

COD PIE. (Economical.)

[COLD MEAT COOKERY.] *Ingredients.*—Any remains of cold cod, 12 oysters, sufficient melted butter to moisten it; mashed potatoes enough to fill up the dish. *Mode.*—Flake the fish from the bone, and carefully take away all the skin. Lay it in a pie-dish, pour over the melted butter and oysters (or oyster sauce, if there is any left), and cover with mashed potatoes. Bake for ½ an hour, and send to table of a nice brown colour. *Time.*—½ hour. *Seasonable* from November to March.

COD, Salt, commonly called "Salt-fish."

Ingredients.—Sufficient water to cover the fish. *Mode.*—Wash the fish, and lay it all night in water, with a ¼ pint of vinegar. When thoroughly soaked, take it out, see that it is perfectly clean, and put it in the fish-kettle with sufficient cold water to cover it. Heat it gradually, but do not let it boil much, or the fish will be hard. Skim well, and when done, drain the fish, and put it on a napkin garnished with hard-boiled eggs cut in rings. *Time.*—About 1 hour. *Average cost*, 6*d.* per lb. *Sufficient* for each person, ¼ lb. *Seasonable* in the spring.

Note.—Serve with egg sauce and parsnips. This is an especial dish on Ash Wednesday.

COD SOUNDS

Should be well soaked in salt and water, and thoroughly washed before dressing them. They are considered a great delicacy, and may either be broiled, fried, or boiled; if they are boiled, mix a little milk with the water.

COD SOUNDS, en Poule.

Ingredients.—For forcemeat, 12 chopped oysters, 3 chopped anchovies, ¼ lb. of bread-crumbs, 1 oz. of butter, 2 eggs, seasoning of salt, pepper, nutmeg, and mace to taste; 4 cod sounds. *Mode.*—Make the forcemeat by mixing the ingredients well together. Wash the sounds, and boil them in milk and water for ½ an hour; take them out, and let them cool. Cover each with a layer of forcemeat, roll them up in a nice form, and skewer them. Rub over with lard, dredge with flour, and cook them gently before the fire in a Dutch oven. *Time.*—1 hour. *Average cost*, 6*d*. per lb.

COD'S HEAD & SHOULDERS.

Ingredients.—Sufficient water to cover the fish; 5 oz. of salt to each gallon of water. *Mode.*—Cleanse the fish thoroughly, and rub a little salt over the thick part and inside of the fish 1 or 2 hours before dressing it, as this very much improves the flavour. Lay it in the fish-kettle, with sufficient cold water to cover it. Be very particular not to pour the water on the fish, as it is liable to break it, and only keep it just simmering. If the water should boil away, add a little by pouring it in at the side of the kettle, and not on the fish. Add salt in the above proportion, and bring it gradually to a boil. Skim very carefully, draw it to the side of the fire, and let it gently simmer till done. Take it out and drain it; serve on a hot napkin, and garnish with cut lemon and horseradish. *Time.*—According to size, ½ an hour, more or less. *Average cost*, from 3*s*. to 6*s*. *Sufficient* for 6 or 8 persons. *Seasonable* from November to March.

Note.—Oyster sauce and plain melted butter should be served with this.

COD'S HEAD & SHOULDERS, to Carve.

First run the knife along the centre of the side of the fish, namely, from *d* to *b*, down to the bone; then carve it in unbroken slices downwards from *d* to *e*, or upwards from *d* to *c*, as shown in the engraving. The carver should ask the guests if they would like a portion of the roe and liver.

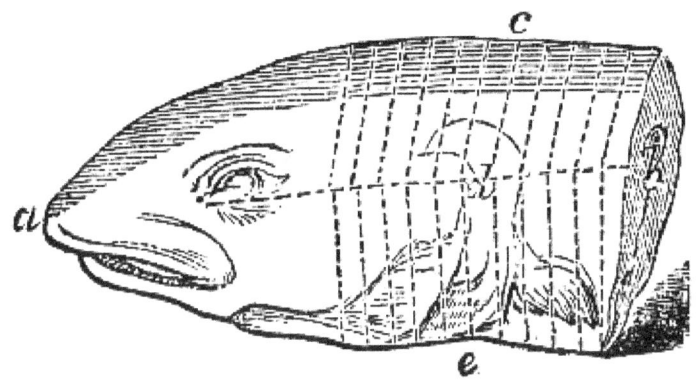

Note.—Of this fish, the parts about the backbone and shoulders are the firmest and most esteemed by connoisseurs. The sound, which lines the fish beneath the backbone, is considered a delicacy, as are also the gelatinous parts about the head and neck.

COFFEE, Essence of.

Ingredients.—To every ¼ lb. of ground coffee allow 1 small teaspoonful of powdered chicory, 3 small teacupfuls, or 1 pint, of water. *Mode.*—Let the coffee be freshly ground, and, if possible, freshly roasted; put it into a percolater, or filter, with the chicory, and pour *slowly* over it the above proportion of boiling water. When it has all filtered through, warm the coffee sufficiently to bring it to the simmering-point, but do not allow it to boil; then filter it a second time, put it into a clean and dry bottle, cork it well, and it will remain good for several days. Two tablespoonfuls of this essence are quite sufficient for a breakfast-cupful of hot milk. This essence will be found particularly useful to those persons who have to rise extremely early; and having only the milk to make boiling, is very easily and quickly prepared. When the essence is bottled, pour another 3 teacupfuls of *boiling* water slowly on the grounds, which, when filtered through, will be a very weak coffee. The next time there is essence to be prepared, make this weak coffee boiling, and pour it on the ground coffee instead of plain water: by this means a better coffee will be obtained. Never throw away the grounds without having made use of them in this manner; and always cork the bottle well that contains this preparation, until the day that it is wanted for making the fresh essence. *Time.*—To be filtered once, then brought to the boiling-point, and filtered again. *Average cost,* with coffee at 1*s*. 8*d*. per lb., 6*d*. *Sufficient.*—Allow 2 tablespoonfuls for a breakfast-cupful of hot milk.

COFFEE, Nutritious.

Ingredients.—½ oz. of ground coffee, 1 pint of milk. *Mode.*—Let the coffee be freshly ground; put it into a saucepan with the milk, which should be made nearly boiling before the coffee is put in, and boil together for 3 minutes; clear it by pouring some of it into a cup, and then back again, and leave it on the hob for a few minutes to settle thoroughly. This coffee may be made still more nutritious by the addition of an egg well beaten, and put into the coffee-cup. *Time.*—5 minutes to boil, 5 minutes to settle. *Sufficient* to make 1 large breakfast-cupful of coffee.

COFFEE, Simple Method of Making.

Ingredients.—Allow ½ oz., or 1 tablespoonful, of coffee to each person; to every oz. allow ½ pint of water. *Mode.*—Have a small iron ring made to fit the top of the coffee-pot inside, and to this ring sew a small muslin bag (the muslin for the purpose must not be too thin). Fit the bag into the pot, warm the pot with some boiling water; throw this away, and put the ground coffee into the bag; pour over as much boiling water as is required, close the lid, and, when all the water has filtered through, remove the bag, and send the coffee to table. Making it in this manner prevents the necessity of pouring the coffee from one vessel to another, which cools and spoils it. The water should be poured on the coffee gradually, so that the infusion may be stronger; and the bag must be well made, that none of the grounds may escape through the seams, and so make the coffee thick and muddy. *Sufficient.*—Allow 1 tablespoonful, or ½ oz., to each person.

COFFEE, to Make.

LOYSEL'S HYDROSTATIC URN.

Ingredients.—Allow ½ oz., or 1 tablespoonful, of ground coffee to each person; to every oz. of coffee allow 1/3 pint of water. *Mode.*—To make coffee good, *it should never be boiled*, but the boiling water merely poured on it, the same as for tea. The coffee should always be purchased in the berry,—if possible, freshly roasted; and it should never be ground long before it is wanted for use. There are very many new kinds of coffee-pots, but the method of making the coffee is nearly always the same, namely, pouring the boiling water on the powder, and allowing it to filter through. Our illustration shows one of Loysel's Hydrostatic Urns, which are admirably adapted for making good and clear coffee, which should be made in the following manner:—Warm the urn with boiling water, remove the lid and movable filter, and place the ground coffee at the bottom of the urn. Put the movable filter over this, and screw the lid, inverted, tightly on the end of the centre pipe. Pour into the inverted lid the above proportion of boiling water, and when all the water so poured has disappeared from the funnel, and made its way down the centre pipe and up again through the ground coffee by *hydrostatic pressure*, unscrew the lid and cover the urn. Pour back direct into the urn, *not through the funnel*, one, two, or three cups, according to the size of the percolater, in order to make the infusion of uniform strength; the contents will then be ready for use, and should run from the tap strong, hot, and clear. The coffee made in these urns generally turns out very good, and there is but one objection to them,—the coffee runs rather slowly from the tap; this is of no consequence where there is a small party, but tedious where there are many persons to provide for. A remedy for this objection may be suggested, namely, to make the coffee very strong, so that not more than 1/3 cup would be required, as the rest would be filled up with milk. Making coffee in filters or percolaters does away with the necessity of using isinglass, white of egg, and various other preparations, to clear it. Coffee should always be served very hot, and, if possible, in the same vessel in which it is made, as pouring it from one pot to another cools, and consequently spoils it. Many persons may think that the proportion of water we have given for each oz. of coffee is rather small; it is so, and the coffee produced from it will be very strong; 1/3 of a cup will be found quite sufficient, which should be filled with nice hot milk, or milk and cream mixed. This is the *café au lait* for which our neighbours over the Channel are so justly celebrated. Should the ordinary method of making coffee be preferred, use double the quantity of water, and, in pouring it into the cups, put in more coffee and less milk. *Sufficient.*—For very good coffee, allow ½ oz., or 1 tablespoonful, to each person.

COFFEE, to Roast. (A French Recipe.)

It being an acknowledged fact that French coffee is decidedly superior to that made in England, and as the roasting of the berry is of great importance to the flavour of the preparation, it will be useful and interesting to know how they manage these things in France. In Paris, there are two houses justly celebrated for the flavour of their coffee,—*La Maison Corcellet* and *La Maison Royer de Chartres*; and to obtain this flavour before roasting, they add to every 3 lbs. of coffee a piece of butter the size of a nut, and a dessertspoonful of powdered sugar: it is then roasted in the usual manner. The addition of the butter and sugar develops the flavour and aroma of the berry; but it must be borne in mind, that the quality of the butter must be of the very best description.

COLLOPS, Scotch.

[COLD MEAT COOKERY.] *Ingredients.*—The remains of cold roast veal, a little butter, flour, ½ pint of water, 1 onion, 1 blade of pounded mace, 1 tablespoonful of lemon-juice, 1-2 teaspoonful of finely-minced lemon-peel, 2 tablespoonfuls of sherry, 1 tablespoonful of mushroom ketchup. *Mode.*—

Cut the veal the same thickness as for cutlets, rather larger than a crown piece; flour the meat well, and fry a light brown in butter; dredge again with flour, and add ½ pint of water, pouring it in by degrees; set it on the fire, and when it boils, add the onion and mace, and let it simmer very gently about ¾ hour; flavour the gravy with lemon-juice, peel, wine, and ketchup, in the above proportion; give one boil, and serve. *Time.*—¾ hour. *Seasonable* from March to October.

COLLOPS, Scotch, White.

[COLD MEAT COOKERY.] *Ingredients.*—The remains of cold roast veal, ½ teaspoonful of grated nutmeg, 2 blades of pounded mace, cayenne and salt to taste, a little butter, 1 dessertspoonful of flour, ¼ pint of water, 1 teaspoonful of anchovy sauce, 1 tablespoonful of lemon-juice, ¼ teaspoonful of lemon-peel, 1 tablespoonful of mushroom ketchup, 3 tablespoonfuls of cream, 1 tablespoonful of sherry. *Mode.*—Cut the veal into thin slices about 3 inches in width; hack them with a knife, and grate on them the nutmeg, mace, cayenne, and salt, and fry them in a little butter. Dish them, and make a gravy in the pan by putting in the remaining ingredients. Give one boil, and pour it over the collops; garnish with lemon and slices of toasted bacon, rolled. Forcemeat balls may be added to this dish. If cream is not at hand, substitute the yolk of an egg beaten up well with a little milk. *Time.*—About 5 or 7 minutes. *Seasonable* from May to October.

COMPÔTE.

A confiture made at the moment of need, and with much less sugar than would be ordinarily put to preserves. They are very wholesome things, suitable to most stomachs which cannot accommodate themselves to raw fruit or a large portion of sugar: they are the happy medium, and far better than ordinary stewed fruit. For Fruit Compôtes refer to the recipes relating to the various Fruits.

CONFECTIONARY.

In speaking of confectionary, it should be remarked that many preparations come under that head; for the various fruits, flowers, herbs, roots, and juices, which, when boiled with sugar, were formerly employed in pharmacy as well as for sweetmeats, were called *confections*, from the Latin word *conficere*, 'to make up;' but the term confectionary embraces a very large class indeed of sweet food, many kinds of which should not be attempted in the ordinary cuisine. The thousand and one ornamental dishes that adorn the tables of the wealthy should be purchased from the confectioner: they cannot profitably be made at home. Apart from these, cakes, biscuits, and tarts, &c., the class of sweetmeats called confections may be thus classified:—1. Liquid confects, or fruits either whole or in pieces, preserved by being immersed in a fluid transparent syrup; as the liquid confects of apricots, green citrons, and many foreign fruits. 2. Dry confects are those which, after having been boiled in the syrup, are taken out and put to dry in an oven, as citron and orange-peel, &c. 3. Marmalade, jams, and pastes, a kind of soft compounds made of the pulp of fruits or other vegetable substances, beat up with sugar or honey; such as oranges, apricots, pears, &c. 4. Jellies are the juices of fruits boiled with sugar to a pretty thick consistency, so as, upon cooling, to form a trembling jelly; as currant, gooseberry, apple jelly, &c. 5. Conserves are a kind of dry confects, made by beating up flowers, fruits, &c., with sugar, not dissolved. 6. Candies are fruits candied over with sugar after having been boiled in the syrup.

COW-HEEL, Fried.

Ingredients.—Ox-feet, the yolk of 1 egg, bread-crumbs, parsley, salt and cayenne to taste, boiling butter. *Mode.*—Wash, scald, and thoroughly clean the feet, and cut them into pieces about 2 inches long; have ready some fine bread-crumbs mixed with a little minced parsley, cayenne, and salt; dip the pieces of heel into the yolk of egg, sprinkle them with the bread-crumbs, and fry them until of a nice brown in boiling butter. *Time.*—¼ hour. *Average cost*, 6*d.* each. *Seasonable* at any time.

Note.—Ox-feet maybe dressed in various ways, stewed in gravy or plainly boiled and served with melted butter. When plainly boiled, the liquor will answer for making sweet or relishing jellies, and also to give richness to soups or gravies.

COW-HEEL STOCK, for Jellies (More Economical than Calf's-Feet).

Ingredients.—2 cow-heels, 3 quarts of water. *Mode.*—Procure 2 heels that have only been scalded, and not boiled; split them in two, and remove the fat between the claws; wash them well in warm water, and put them into a saucepan with the above proportion of cold water; bring it gradually to boil, remove all the scum as it rises, and simmer the heels gently from 7 to 8 hours, or until the liquor is reduced one-half; then strain it into a basin, measuring the quantity, and put it in a cool place. Clarify it in the same manner as calf's-feet stock, using, with the other ingredients, about ½ oz. of isinglass to each quart. This stock should be made the day before it is required for use. Two dozen shank-bones of mutton, boiled for 6 or 7 hours, yield a quart of strong firm stock. They should be put on in 2 quarts of water, which should be reduced one-half. Make this also the day before it is required. *Time.*—7 to 8 hours to boil the cow-heels, 6 to 7 hours to boil the shank-bones. *Average cost*, from 4*d.* to 6*d.* each. *Sufficient.*—2 cow-heels should make 3 pints of stock. *Seasonable* at any time.

COWSLIP WINE.

Ingredients.—To every gallon of water allow 3 lbs. of lump sugar, the rind of 2 lemons, the juice of 1, the rind and juice of 1 Seville orange, 1 gallon of cowslip pips. To every 4½ gallons of wine allow 1 bottle of brandy. *Mode.*—Boil the sugar and water together for ½ hour, carefully removing all the scum as it rises. Pour this boiling liquor on the orange and lemon-rinds and the juice, which should be strained; when milk-warm, add the cowslip pips or flowers, picked from the stalks and seeds; and to 9 gallons of wine 3 tablespoonfuls of good fresh brewers' yeast. Let it ferment 3 or 4 days, then put all together in a cask with the brandy, and let it remain for 2 months, when bottle it off for use. *Time.*—To be boiled ½ hour; to ferment 3 or 4 days; to remain in the cask 2 months. *Average cost*, exclusive of the cowslips, which may be picked in the fields, 2*s.* 9*d.* per gallon. *Seasonable.* Make this in April or May.

CRAB, to Choose.

The middle-sized crab is the best; and the crab, like the lobster, should be judged by its weight; for if light, it is watery.

CRAB, to Dress.

Ingredients.—1 crab, 2 tablespoonfuls of vinegar, 1 ditto of oil; salt, white pepper, and cayenne, to taste. *Mode.*—Empty the shells, and thoroughly mix the meat with the above ingredients, and put it in the large shell. Garnish with slices of cut lemon and parsley. The quantity of oil may be increased when it is much liked. *Average cost*, from 10*d.* to 2*s. Seasonable* all the year; but not so good in May, June, and July. *Sufficient* for 3 persons.

CRAB, Hot.

Ingredients.—1 crab, nutmeg, salt and pepper to taste, 3 oz. of butter, ¼ lb. of bread-crumbs, 3 tablespoonfuls of vinegar. *Mode.*—After having boiled the crab, pick the meat out from the shells, and mix with it the nutmeg and seasoning. Cut up the butter in small pieces, and add the bread-crumbs and vinegar. Mix altogether, put the whole in the large shell, and brown before the fire or with a salamander. *Time.*—1 hour. *Average cost*, from 10*d.* to 2*s. Sufficient* for 3 persons, *Seasonable* all the year; but not so good in May, June, and July.

CRAB SAUCE, for Fish (equal to Lobster Sauce).

Ingredients.—1 crab; salt, pounded mace, and cayenne to taste; ½ pint of melted butter made with milk. *Mode.*—Choose a nice fresh crab, pick all the meat away from the shell, and cut it into small square pieces. Make ½ pint of melted butter, put in the fish and seasoning; let it gradually warm through, and simmer for 2 minutes: it should not boil. *Average cost*, 1*s.* 2*d.*

CRAYFISH.

Crayfish should be thrown into boiling water, to which has been added a good seasoning of salt and a little vinegar. When done, which will be in ¼ hour, take them out and drain them. Let them cool, arrange them on a napkin, and garnish with plenty of double parsley.

Note.—This fish is frequently used for garnishing boiled turkey, boiled fowl, calf's head, turbot, and all kinds of boiled fish.

CRAYFISH, Potted.

Ingredients.—100 crayfish; pounded mace, pepper, and salt to taste; 2 oz. butter. *Mode.*—Boil the fish in salt and water, pick out all the meat, and pound it in a mortar to a paste. Whilst pounding, add the butter gradually, and mix in the spice and seasoning. Put it in small pots, and pour over it clarified butter, carefully excluding the air. *Time.*—15 minutes to boil the crayfish. *Average cost*, 2s. 9d. *Seasonable* all the year.

CRAYFISH SOUP.

Ingredients.—50 crayfish, ¼ lb. of butter, 6 anchovies, the crumb of 1 French roll, a little lobster-spawn, seasoning to taste, 2 quarts of medium stock, or fish stock. *Mode.*—Shell the crayfish, and put the fish between two plates until they are wanted; pound the shells in a mortar with the butter and anchovies; when well beaten, add a pint of stock, and simmer for ¾ of an hour. Strain it through a hair sieve, put the remainder of the stock to it, with the crumb of the roll; give it one boil, and rub it through a tammy, with the lobster-spawn. Put in the fish, but do not let the soup boil after it has been rubbed through the tammy. If necessary, add seasoning. *Time.*—1½ hour. *Average cost*, 2s. 3d. or 1s. 9d. per quart. *Sufficient* for 8 persons. *Seasonable* from January to July.

CREAM à la VALOIS.

Ingredients.—4 sponge-cakes, jam, ¾ pint of cream, sugar to taste, the juice of ½ lemon, ¼ glass of sherry, 1¼ oz. of isinglass. *Mode.*—Cut the sponge-cakes into thin slices, place two together with preserve between them, and pour over them a small quantity of sherry mixed with a little brandy. Sweeten and flavour the cream with the lemon-juice and sherry; add the isinglass, which should be dissolved in a little water, and beat up the cream well. Place a little in an oiled mould; arrange the pieces of cake in the cream, then fill the mould with the remainder, let it cool, and turn it out on a dish. By oiling the mould the cream will have a much smoother appearance, and will turn out more easily than when merely dipped in cold water. *Average cost,* 3s. 6d. *Sufficient* to fill a 1½ pint mould. *Seasonable* at any time.

CREAM CHEESE.

Cream cheese should be served on a d'oyley, and garnished either with water-cresses or parsley; of the former, a plentiful supply should be given, as they add greatly to the appearance of the dish, besides improving the flavour of the cheese.

CREAM, Devonshire.

The milk should stand 24 hours in the winter, half that time when the weather is very warm. The milkpan is then set on a stove, and should there remain until the milk is quite hot; but it must not boil, or there will be a thick skin on the surface. When it is sufficiently done the undulations on the surface look thick, and small rings appear. The time required for scalding cream depends on the size of the pan and the heat of the fire, but the slower it is done the better. The pan should be placed in the dairy when the cream is sufficiently scalded, and skimmed the following day. This cream is so much esteemed that it is sent to the London markets in small square tins, and is exceedingly delicious eaten with fresh fruit. In Devonshire, butter is made from this cream, and is usually very firm.

CREAM, Italian.

Ingredients.—½ pint of milk, ½ pint of cream, sugar to taste, 1 oz. of isinglass, 1 lemon, the yolks of 4 eggs. *Mode.*—Put the cream and milk into a saucepan, with sugar to sweeten, and the lemon-rind. Boil until the milk is well flavoured, then strain it into a basin and add the beaten yolks of eggs. Put this mixture into a jug, place the jug in a saucepan of boiling water over the fire, and stir the contents until they thicken, but do not allow them to boil. Take the cream off the fire, stir in the lemon-juice and isinglass, which should be melted, and whip well; fill a mould, place it in ice if at hand, and, when set, turn it out on a dish, and garnish as taste may dictate. The mixture may be whipped and drained, and then put into small glasses, when this mode of serving is preferred. *Time.*—From 5 to 8 minutes to stir the mixture in the jug. *Average cost,* with the best isinglass, 2*s.* 6*d. Sufficient* to fill 1½ pint mould. *Seasonable* at any time.

CREAM SAUCE, for Fish or White Dishes.

Ingredients.—1/3 pint of cream, 2 oz. of butter, 1 teaspoonful of flour, salt and cayenne to taste; when liked, a small quantity of pounded mace or lemon-juice. *Mode.*—Put the butter in a very clean saucepan, dredge in the flour, and keep shaking round till the butter is melted. Add the seasoning and cream, and stir the whole till it boils; let it just simmer for 5 minutes, when add either pounded mace or lemon-juice to taste to give it a flavour. *Time.*—5 minutes to simmer. *Average cost* for this quantity, 7*d.*

Note.—This sauce may be flavoured with very finely-shredded shalot.

CREAM, Stone, of tous les Mois.

Ingredients.—½ lb. of preserve, 1 pint of milk, 2 oz. of lump sugar, 1 heaped tablespoonful of tous les mois, 3 drops of essence of cloves, 3 drops of almond-flavouring. *Mode.*—Place the preserve at the bottom of a glass dish; put the milk into a lined saucepan, with the sugar, and make it boil. Mix to a smooth batter the tous les mois with a very little cold milk; stir it briskly into the boiling milk, add the flavouring, and simmer for 2 minutes. When rather cool, but before turning solid, pour the cream over the jam, and ornament it with strips of red-currant jelly or preserved fruit. *Time.*—2 minutes. *Average cost,* 10*d. Sufficient* for 4 or 5 persons. *Seasonable* at any time.

CREAM, Swiss.

Ingredients.—¼ lb. of macaroons or 6 small sponge-cakes, sherry, 1 pint of cream, 5 oz. of lump sugar, 2 large tablespoonfuls of arrowroot, the rind of 1 lemon, the juice of ½ lemon, 3 tablespoonfuls of milk. *Mode.*—Lay the macaroons or sponge-cakes in a glass dish, and pour over them as much sherry as will cover them, or sufficient to soak them well. Put the cream into a lined saucepan, with the sugar and lemon-rind, and let it remain by the side of the fire until the cream is well flavoured, when take out the lemon-rind. Mix the arrowroot smoothly with the cold milk; add this to the cream, and let it boil gently for about 3 minutes, keeping it well stirred. Take it off the fire, stir till nearly cold, when add the lemon-juice, and pour the whole over the cakes. Garnish the cream with strips of angelica, or candied citron cut thin, or bright-coloured jelly or preserve. This cream is exceedingly delicious, flavoured with vanilla instead of lemon: when this flavouring is used the sherry may be omitted, and the mixture poured over the *dry* cakes. *Time.*—About ½ hour to infuse the lemon-rind; 5 minutes to boil the cream. *Average cost*, with cream at 1s. per pint, 3s. *Sufficient* for 5 or 6 persons. *Seasonable* at any time.

CREAM, Vanilla.

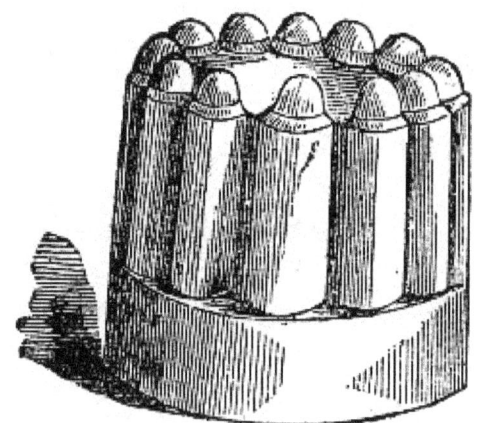

VANILLA-CREAM MOULD.

Ingredients.—1 pint of milk, the yolks of 8 eggs, 6 oz. of sugar, 1 oz. of isinglass, flavouring to taste of essence of vanilla. *Mode.*—Put the milk and sugar into a saucepan, and let it get hot over a slow fire; beat up the yolks of the eggs, to which add gradually the sweetened milk; flavour the whole with essence of vanilla, put the mixture into a jug, and place this jug in a saucepan of boiling water. Stir the contents with a wooden spoon one way until the mixture thickens, but do not allow it to boil, or it will be full of lumps. Take it off the fire; stir in the isinglass, which should be previously dissolved in about ¼ pint of water, and boiled for 2 or 3 minutes; pour the cream into an oiled mould, put it in a cool place to set, and turn it out carefully on a dish. Instead of using the essence of vanilla, a pod may be boiled in the milk until the flavour is well extracted. A pod, or a pod and a half, will be found sufficient for the above proportion of ingredients. *Time.*

—About 10 minutes to stir the mixture. *Average cost*, with the best isinglass, 2*s.* 6*d.* *Sufficient* to fill a quart mould. *Seasonable* at any time.

CREAM, Whipped, for putting on Trifles, serving in Glasses, &c.

Ingredients.—To every pint of cream allow 3 oz. of pounded sugar, 1 glass of sherry or any kind of sweet white wine, the rind of ½ lemon, the white of 1 egg. *Mode.*—Rub the sugar on the lemon-rind, and pound it in a mortar until quite fine, and beat up the white of the egg until quite stiff; put the cream into a large bowl, with the sugar, wine, and beaten egg, and whip it to a froth; as fast as the froth rises take it off with a skimmer, and put it on a sieve to drain in a cool place. This should be made the day before it is wanted, as the whip is then so much firmer. The cream should be whipped in a cool place, and in summer over ice, if it is obtainable. A plain whipped cream may be served on a glass dish, and garnished with strips of angelica, or pastry-leaves, or pieces of bright-coloured jelly: it makes a very pretty addition to the supper-table. *Time.*—About 1 hour to whip the cream. *Average cost*, with cream at 1*s.* per pint, 1*s.* 9*d.* *Sufficient* for 1 dish or 1 trifle. *Seasonable* at any time.

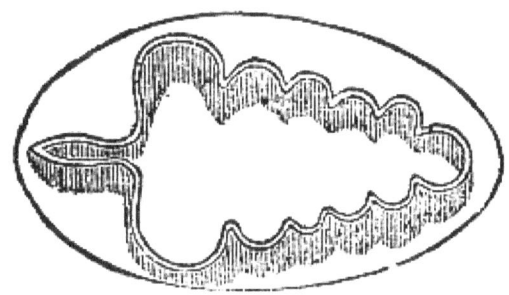

PASTRY-LEAF.

CRUMPETS.

These are made in the same manner as muffins, only, in making the mixture, let it be more like batter than dough. Let it rise for about ½ hour; pour it into iron rings, which should be ready on a hot-plate; bake them, and when one side appears done, turn them quickly on the other. *To toast them*, have ready a very *bright clear* fire; put the crumpet on a toasting-fork, and hold it before the fire, *not too close,* until it is nicely brown on one side, but do not allow it to blacken; turn it, and brown the other side; then spread it with good butter, cut it in half, and, when all are done, pile them on a hot dish, and send them quickly to table. Muffins and crumpets should always be served on separate dishes, and both toasted and served as expeditiously as possible. *Time.*—From 10 to 15 minutes to bake them. *Sufficient.*—Allow 2 crumpets to each person.

CRUST, Butter, for Boiled Puddings.

Ingredients.—To every lb. of flour allow 6 oz. of butter, ½ pint of water. *Mode.*—With a knife, work the flour to a smooth paste with ½ pint of water; roll the crust out rather thin; place the butter over it in small pieces, dredge lightly over it some flour, and fold the paste over; repeat the rolling once more, and the crust will be ready for use. It may be enriched by adding another 2 oz. of butter; but, for ordinary purposes, the above quantity will be found quite sufficient. *Average cost*, 6*d.* per lb.

CRUST, Common, for Raised Pies.

Ingredients.—To every lb. of flour allow ½ pint of water, 1½ oz. of butter, 1½ oz. of lard, ½ saltspoonful of salt. *Mode.*—Put into a saucepan the water; when it boils, add the butter and lard, and when these are melted, make a hole in the middle of the flour; pour in the water gradually, beat it well with a wooden spoon, and be particular in not making the paste too soft. When it is well mixed, knead it with the hands until quite stiff, dredging a little flour over the paste and board to prevent them from sticking. When it is well kneaded, place it before the fire, with a cloth covered over it, for a few minutes; it will then be more easily worked into shape. This paste does not taste so nicely as a richer one, but it is worked with greater facility, and answers just as well for raised pies, for the crust is seldom eaten. *Average cost*, 5*d.* per lb.

CRUST, Dripping, for Kitchen Puddings, Pies, &c.

Ingredients.—To every lb. of flour allow 6 oz. of clarified beef dripping, ½ pint of water. *Mode.*—After having clarified the dripping, weigh it, and to every lb. of flour allow the above proportion of dripping. With a knife, work the flour into a smooth paste with the water, rolling it out three times, each time placing on the crust 2 oz. of the dripping broken into small pieces. If this paste is lightly made, if good dripping is used, and *not too much of it*, it will be found good; and by the addition of two tablespoonfuls of fine moist sugar, it may be converted into a common short crust for fruit pies. *Average cost*, 4*d.* per lb.

CRUST, Lard or Flead.

Ingredients.—To every lb. of flour allow ½ lb. of lard or flead, ½ pint of water, ½ saltspoonful of salt. *Mode.*—Clear the flead from skin, and slice it into thin flakes; rub it into the flour, add the salt, and work the whole into a smooth paste, with the above proportion of water; fold the paste over two or three times, beat it well with the rolling-pin, roll it out, and it will be ready for use. The crust made from this will be found extremely light, and may be made into cakes or tarts; it may also be very much enriched by adding more flead to the same proportion of flour. *Average cost*, 8*d.* per lb.

CRUST, Suet, for Pies or Puddings.

Ingredients.—To every lb. of flour allow 5 or 6 oz. of beef suet, ½ pint of water. *Mode.*—Free the suet from skin and shreds, chop it extremely fine, and rub it well into the flour; work the whole to a smooth paste with the above proportion of water; roll it out, and it is ready for use. This crust is quite rich enough for ordinary purposes, but when a better one is desired, use from ½ to ¾ lb. of suet to every lb. of flour. Some cooks, for rich crusts, pound the suet in a mortar, with a small quantity of butter. It should then be laid on the paste in small pieces, the same as for puff-crust, and will be found exceedingly nice for hot tarts. 5 oz. of suet to every lb. of flour will make a very good crust; and even ¼ lb, will answer very well for children, or where the crust is wanted very plain. *Average cost*, 5*d.* per lb.

CRUST, Common Short.

Ingredients.—To every lb. of flour allow 2 oz. of sifted sugar, 3 oz. of butter, about ½ pint of boiling milk. *Mode.*—Crumble the butter into the flour as finely as possible, add the sugar, and work the whole up to a smooth paste with the boiling milk. Roll it out thin, and bake in a moderate oven. *Average cost*, 6*d.* per lb.

CRUST, Very good Short for Fruit Tarts.

Ingredients.—To every lb. of flour allow ½ or ¾ lb. of butter, 1 tablespoonful of sifted sugar, 1/3 pint of water. *Mode.*—Rub the butter into the flour, after having ascertained that the latter is perfectly dry; add the sugar, and mix the whole into a stiff paste with about 1/3 pint of water. Roll it out two or three times, folding the paste over each time, and it will be ready for use. *Average cost*, 1*s*. 1*d*. per lb.

CRUST, Another good Short.

Ingredients.—To every lb. of flour allow 8 oz. of butter, the yolks of 2 eggs, 2 oz. of sifted sugar, about ¼ pint of milk. *Mode.*—Rub the butter into the flour, add the sugar, and mix the whole as lightly as possible to a smooth paste, with the yolks of the eggs well beaten, and the milk. The proportion of the latter ingredient must be judged of by the size of the eggs; if these are large so much will not be required, and more if the eggs are smaller. *Average cost*, 1*s*. per lb.

CUCUMBER SAUCE.

Ingredients.—3 or 4 cucumbers, 2 oz. of butter, 6 tablespoonfuls of brown gravy. *Mode.*—Peel the cucumbers, quarter them, and take out the seeds; cut them into small pieces, put them in a cloth, and rub them well to take out the water that hangs about them. Put the butter in a saucepan, add the cucumbers, and shake them over a sharp fire until they are of a good colour; then pour over them the gravy, mixed with the cucumbers, and simmer gently for 10 minutes, when it will be ready to serve. *Time.*—Altogether, ½ hour.

www.ingramcontent.com/pod-product-compliance
Lightning Source LLC
Chambersburg PA
CBHW081624100526
44590CB00021B/3591